Kids
FOR THE
WORLD

A Guidebook for Children's Mission Resources

GERRY DUECK

William Carey Library
PASADENA, CALIFORNIA

Published by
William Carey Library
P.O. Box 40129
Pasadena, CA 91114
(818) 798-0819

ISBN 0-87808-768-0

CONTENTS

Introduction   v

How to Use This Guidebook   vii

Part I: Resources

1. Curricula   3
2. Books   14
3. Stories   28
4. Activities   31
5. Visual Aids   38
6. Audio-Visuals   46
7. Songs, Music   51
8. Index of Places   58
9. Index of Children's Mission Resource Publishers/Suppliers   71
10. Index of Missionaries   96
11. Index of Resource Persons   104

Part II: Samples

12. Curricular Outlines   113
13. Lessons   125
14. Activities   140
15. Supplementary Readings   153

INTRODUCTION

I did not so much write this book as watch it evolve. The saying "Necessity is the mother of invention" seems to apply very aptly to the development of what you now hold in your hands.

What started out as a 24-page list of materials published by a few publishers around 1985 grew to a larger list in 1986, then the first edition of the yellow book, *Resources and Lessons*, in 1987, followed by the yellow *Kids For the World* in 1988, which included a few lesson samples. The blue *Kids For the World* was then published in 1990, after which I wrote three Supplements. I gained much insight by teaching "world view" and "hidden peoples" classes in many churches, children's groups, and the William Carey Academy on the campus of the U.S. Center for World Mission. These became, you might say, a laboratory in which I could test many materials and methods. The "Necessity . . ." has till been urgent upon me, so after many delays, many requests for the book, and much research, another edition has again developed.

This edition has all NEW lessons in the Curricula Outline Section. All publishers have been re-checked for corrections and additions of addresses and phone numbers, and FAX numbers have been added where known. For convenience, the Country and People Group Indices have been enlarged and made more complete. Supplemental Readings are NEW. Part II Stories Section and Coloring Pages have been eliminated, since there are adequate sources of these listed in the book. I hope you will find this edition much more helpful than the previous one. Changes in information come to me almost daily, but I have made diligent effort to be as accurate as possible up to the date of publishing.

I'm indebted to the children whom I've taught, who have helped me discover so many things. I'm grateful to the people who helped me with the original book, when I was just a "beginner" on the computer. I'm so grateful to my husband, Vern, who patiently encouraged and prayed for me. The people at my publisher, William Carey, Library (especially Ernie, Lydia, Dave and Jone) have challenged, encouraged, and urged me. Last, but not least, I give glory to my Lord who patiently "nudged" me into this and guided me by his Holy Spirit. He is my companion and guide each time I prepare material.

GLORY BE TO GOD!

Gerry Dueck

How to Use This Guidebook

The *Resources* Sections include lists of all manner of resources you may wish to use in teaching missions to young people. These materials are organized by type, then alphabetically within type. Listings in these sections follow a standard form:

Title. Author(s). Description. Price. Publisher/distributor. (Target Age.)

Target ages are coded as follows:

P = Pre-school and Primary (through 3rd Grade)

I = Intermediate (Grades 4 through 6)

J = Junior High (Grades 6 through 9)

S = Senior High (Grades 10-12)

A = Adult

There are also four cross-indices. When you want an item that deals with a particular subject, this is where you'll want to look first. Are you interested in a country? A place? A people group? Do you want a missionary biography? Take a look at the appropriate index.

Finally, there is a listing of publishers and distributors. Looking through this list you can get a quick idea of who tends to specialize in missions-oriented materials for children. The list of materials after each publisher/distributor/s name only includes items listed in *Kids for the World.* You can be almost assured that, especially for publishers/distributors who have many items after their names, if you write them, you can discover new additions or items I have not reviewed.

Immediately following the publishers/distributors listing, there is another list of resource persons you may want to call on for suggestions or help in creating a mission program of your own.

I hope you find the Curricula Lesson Outlines helpful. Use them or modify them as you see fit.

As a reference work, this volume will be updated from time to time. A supplement will be printed approximately once a year. If you desire such an update, send in the coupon below. Mail to Children's Missions Resource Center, 1605 Elizabeth Street, Pasadena, CA 91104.

- -

Gerry,

Yes, I'm interested in supplements. Please put my name on the list for___ the next supplement/ __ all future supplements. I understand the costs will vary and I will be billed.

Name:_____

Address: _____

_____ Zip _____

PART I

RESOURCES

1

CURRICULA

A Trip to the Land of the Rising Sun. Cheryl Barton. A complete curriculum on Japan. Five lessons and all related activities and songs. $3.00 + S & H. Missions Education. (I)

"Adventure in Brazil." A Fisherkid's Club missionary lesson plan book to accompany the Flashcard story, "Adventures in Brazil" available from Bible Visuals. Each lesson includes pre-session activities, story and song time, craft time, verse time, snack time, and closing activities. Order story from Bible Visuals, Inc. and lesson plan book from Acorn Children's Publications. $8.50. (P,I)

Adventures in Peru and Bolivia. Dondeena Caldwell. A complete curriculum. Five lessons and all related activities and songs. $2.50 + shipping and handling. Missions Education. (I)

Aki and the Banner of Names. Atsuko Goda Lolling. Learn from nine-year-old Aki and other stories about children in Japan, their families, celebrations, and customs. $4.95. Get optional **Teachers' Guide** to this book, to make it a complete course. Includes experiences and activities. $5.95. From Friendship Press. (P,I)

An American Child Visits Japan. Cheryl Barton. A complete curriculum. Five lessons and all related activities and songs. $3.00 + S & H. Missions Education. (P)

Animal Crackers. A curriculum/project featuring five 45-minute sessions for ages 3-adult, focused on Hunger and the Bible, Animals, People, The Environment, and Passing on the Gift. Allows students to raise money to send an HPI animal to a hungry family. Each packet includes a leader's guide, world hunger facts, animal fact sheets and activities, Bible passages, games and a poster. Write for free guidebook to: Heifer Project International.

Arabic Adventure. Dondeena Caldwell. A complete curriculum containing five lessons and all related activities and songs. $3.50 plus S & H. From Missions Education. (I)

Around the World With Jesus. This creative curriculum for VBS stimulates the imagination, presenting the gospel and missions, using games, refreshments, crafts, decorations, daily lessons, and teacher's guide. As children "travel" to India, Nigeria, China, Canada and Columbia, they learn that God wants them to obey Him and tell others about His Love. Great for 5-day clubs and camp also (1991 Edition). David C. Cook Publishing Co., also from One Way Street ($39.95).

Back Home In JAPAN. Melissa Howell. A student fun book for ages 5-10, about a missionary family living in Japan, full of action pictures to color, a story to enjoy, puzzles to solve. The Parent/Teacher's Guide has a five-day plan with 32 pages of extra activities, a song, recipe, game, patterns and more. Student book, $4.50 and Teacher's Guide, $2.75. From OMF BOOKS.

Building Your Temple, With Child To Child. Rosemary Rinker. 13 lessons on primary health care topics applying a spiritual lesson with each. Each unit (lesson) contains a short situation story, the physical teaching, and the spiritual application with Bible study, memory verse, activity, and songs. Some of the topics are Our Nutrition, Caring For our Eyes, Keeping Our Water Clean, Learning About First Aid, Immunizations, AIDS, and more. It is based on peer-to-peer training, its main purpose is for discipleship of children and young people in developing nations. It has been used by YWAM's King's Kids successfully, in orphanages and playgrounds in Nigeria and Ukraine. Contact University of the Nations, School of Primary Health Care.

BGMC Missions education Curriculum. A children's Missions education program used by and available from the Assemblies of God, for preschool and elementary children. A new packet for each quarter, containing missionary stories, learning activities, missionary information pages, and creative ideas. Any group may write for information to BGMC, Sunday School Promotion and Training Department. (See Activities, Fund Raising Projects)

• **Children Caring for Children Ministry.** Take children around the world with Missions projects and material for five lessons. Includes stories and large picture posters for the following countries: China, Brazil, Philippines, Romania and Russia/Ukraine. Object: to raise money to provide "a Bible for every Bibleless home in the world." Indicate which country—each can be had separately. Included in each program kit are five exciting stories, five poster-sized photos, a folder containing discussion topics, a progress chart, and a canister bank. One video per country is optional and extra. Program kits are FREE, but a donation of what the children have raised is requested, and a $5.00 S&H fee to Children Caring for Children, The Bible League. (Also see Activities, Projects, & Videos) (P,I)

Children of the Bible Kit. For VBS, children's church, or Sunday School. Contains 5-lesson "Children of the Bible" flashcard story, 5-lesson "Ringu of India's Forest" flashcard story, 5 visualized Bible verses, and "Yes I Can" visualized song. $20.99. CEF Press. (P,I)

• **Children of the World Travel Agency.** Anita Cadonau. 14-lesson Mission curriculum takes children each week on an imaginary trip to another country where they learn about the land, the people, and universal need all men have for a Savior. Using an airport/airplane format for each lesson, it includes many visual aids, craft suggestions, reproducible pages, and songs along with the lesson plans. The program is $17.95. Contact Anita Cadonau, c/o Beaverton Foursquare Church (see Resource Persons).

Children's Church Primary Programs. Revised three-year course of 156 programs, 63 of which are either specifically missions, missions-related, or cross-cultural. Reproducible worksheets and craft patterns included. All younger elementary level. Call for prices. All three available from Scripture Press Publications Inc.

Year One (1989): Contains two units about missionary work and family life in Japan, France, and Taiwan.

Year Two (1990): Six programs in a unit called "A Mission for Everyone" concern the history and future of missionary life and work in the USA and Colombia.Includes studies about Bible-time missionaries as well as Hudson Taylor and William Carey, and a study of the Great Commission.

Year Three (1991): Includes a unit entitled "A Day in the Life of a Missionary," and contains lessons about Zimbabwe, Thailand, the Philippines, Greece, Israel, and the ministry of the OM ship Logos.

Children's Mission Sermons. Karen Robertson. Titles: "Good News," "Building God's House," "St. Patrick," "Christopher Columbus," and "Lift High the Cross." Each has materials, suggestions, memory verse, activities and story. All five: $3.00, + postage. Children's Mission Resource Center. (P,I)

Children's Missionary Conferences. How-to-do-it ideas and suggestions. Contains songs, memory verses, illustrated lessons, a few visuals; no pictures or stories. Available in Spanish. $4.75. Lakeland Bible Mission, Inc. (P,I)

Children's Missions Curriculum. Written especially for Christian school use. Contains stories of famous missionaries in history. Betty Paul (see Resource Persons). (P,I)

Choices and Other Stories From the Caribbean (Teachers' Guide). Doris Lou Willis. Background information, activity and worship guides, songs and questions for discussion of the stories in **Choices**. Six-session format, with preparation suggestions for the teacher. Stories about the lives of children in Cuba, Haiti, St. Vincent, Guyana and Jamaica. $5.95. (See Stories for book.) Friendship Press. (P,I)

Courage For a Cross. Leslie Merlin. In six lessons, children learn about Sergei, a talented gymnast in Russia. Exciting adventure awaits Sergei as he figure out what it means to be Christian in a land where sharing one's faith was difficult at one time. $3.95. **Teacher's Guide** available which offers six well-organized lesson plans, Bible study, songs, crafts and games. Included is a soundsheet and the 10-frame fimship. $9.95. Both from Friendship Press. (P,I)

Crickets and Corn. Peg Back. A complete curriculum about Indians of North America. Five lessons and all related activities and songs. $3.00 + S & H. Missions Education. (I)

Days of Discovery. A five-dayVacation Bible School Missions Kit with video. Follow the adventures of Jeremy and Rachel as they stumble upon a giant mechanical "dish" and then meet a kindly gentleman who explains the "dish" and the worldwide ministry of Good News Productions, International. Includes a video with five segments (approx. 8 minutes each), bulletin board photos, and a list of possible projects for radio and TV broadcasting the Gospel. Contact Good News Productions, International.

Destination 2000 A.D. By Jill Harris and Bob Sjogren. A children's Training Curriculum, designed to teach missions to children in an exciting fun-packed way! Destination 2000 Teacher's Training Curriculum videos are optional. The first part is a 13-lesson format focused on 1) God's Missionary plan throughout the Bible, and 2) the major blocks of Unreached People Groups. The second part uses D2000 Teaching Components to emphasize God's focus in the Bible of "Blessed To Be A Blessing," action steps, songs, games, and crafts. The third part is the M and M Kid's Manual (to copy) for kids. The full video kit includes videos, manual and slides costs $99.95, and the Teacher's Training Manual with slides only costs $24.95. Available from Frontiers. (P & I)

Developing World Christians. By Marguerite Harrell, M. Ed. A nine-lesson curriculum, each in a separate booklet, but put together in a 3-ring binder. Covers topics ranging from "Who Is A Missionary?" to "What are the Various Types of Missionary Service?" Each lesson includes a suggested song, teacher's guide, activity period suggestion, memory verse, story time, prayer time,project time, and closing suggestions. Write for cost and information to Marguerite Harrell (see Resource Persons). (P & I)

"Devil-Kings and Cannibals." A Shining Star Club and/or Fisherkid's Club Missionary Lesson Plan book to accompany the missionary story, "Devil-Kings and Cannibals" from

Child Evangelism Fellowship Press. Contains the story of John Paton. Each lesson includes pre-session activities, story and song time, craft time, verse time, snack time, and closing activities. Order Story from CEF Press and Lesson Plan book from Acorn Children's Publications. Specify Shining Star (Beginners) $6.50, OR Fisherkid's Club(Primaries) $8.50. (P,I)

Escape By Night. An excellent, complete missions education curriculum about China. It is an exciting adventure of Mui's flight from China, based on true accounts of families who have fled China to live in refugee areas of Macao and Hong Kong. Unit includes seven-part story, 16 poster-size color photos, worksheet, cultural activities, and a map of China. $24.95 plus $2.00 postage and handling. Crossroads Publications. (P,I)

Feed My People. Six lessons designed to communicate with children about hunger and poverty in the world. Teacher's guides include reproducible pages, $5.95 each, Primary #242, Junior #243, Family #244. Video #241, $9.95. Available from Kids Can Make A Difference.

Flights For Kids (MAF Curriculum). Gloria Graham. Three self-contained packets for three distinct age groups: K-1st grade, 2nd-4th, and 5th-6th. Each contains: 1) 5 lessons with teacher's guides; 2) student materials including handouts, Co-Pilot Certificates, MAF cut-out plane, fund-raising project; 3) 1 Cessna 206 poster and more. Visit various countries and the MAF missionaries. Donation of $6 is requested. "Flights For Kids" video is optional and contains three five-minute segments, showing some of the world's most remote areas. Video also $6 donation. Order both from MAF, Gloria Graham—Flights For Kids Coordinator.

Foreign and Home Mission Studies Teaching Guide for Older Preschoolers 1992-93. Activities, games, teaching ideas for giving preschoolers a glimpse of missions. (WMU) #6299-08. $1.75. Order or purchase from any Baptist Book Store Center.

Friends of India. Jan Hill. Part of Southern Baptist 1992 Foreign Mission Study. Tells about William Carey and other missionaries. For grades 4-6. Need to get Teaching Guide for teaching it. #5438-92. $2.85. **Teaching Guide.** (WMU) #6297-87. $1.50. **Jesus Loves Me, Too** (Audiocassette for grades 1-6—see "Let's Go to India.") Order or purchase both from any Baptist Book Store Center.

"George Mueller" (Lessons). A Shining Star Club Missionary Lesson Plan book to accompany the missionary story, "George Mueller" from Acorn Children's Publications. Each lesson includes pre-session activities, story and song time, craft time, verse time, snack time, and closing activities. Order both story and lesson plan book from Acorn Children's Publications. (See Stories) $8.50. (P,I)

"Go Ye." A Fisherkid's Club missionary lesson plan book to accompany the story, "Go Ye," available separately from Acorn Children's Publications. Each lesson includes pre-session activities, story and song time, craft time, verse time, snack time, and closing activities. Order both story and lessons from Acorn Children's Publications. $8.50. (P,I)

"Hudson Taylor." A Shining Star Club and/or Fishserkid's Club Missionary Lesson Plan book to accompany the missionary story, "Hudson Taylor" from Child Evangelism Fellowship Press. Each lesson includes pre-session activities, story and song time, craft time, verse time, snack time, and closing activities. Order story from CEF Press and lesson plan book from Acorn Children's Publications. Specify Shining Star Club (Beginners) $6.50, or Fisherkid's Club (Primaries) $8.50. (P,I)

I Am Important. Dondeena Caldwell. A complete curriculum on Mexican-Americans. Five lessons and all related activities and songs. $2.50 + S & H. Missions Education. (P)

"I Dare." A Shining Star Club and/or Fisherkid's Club Missionary Lesson Plan book to accompany the missionary story, "I Dare" from Child Evangelism Fellowship Press. Contains the story of Amy Carmichel. Each lesson includes pre-session activities, story and song time, craft time, verse time, snack time, and closing activities. Order story from CEF Press and lesson plan book from Acorn Children's Publications. Specify Shining Star Club (Beginners) $6.50, or Fisherkid's Club (Primaries) $8.50. (P,I)

Indonesia: Islands of Flowers, Elephants, and Change Children's Packet. William McElrath and Barbara Wilkinson. The complete 1993 teaching kit containing games, stories, pictures, and activities about the excitement and change in Indonesia. #6381-16. $7.95. From Baptist Book near you, or Baptist Book Order Store in Nashville, Tennessee. (P,I)

Is a Missionary? #1. Teaches Bible basis for Missions. May be used in Children's Missionary Conference, Sunday School class, VBS, or Children's Church. Contains songs, memory verses, illustrated lessons, a few visuals; no pictures or stories. $10.79, includes tax and shipping. Lakeland Bible Mission, Inc. (P,I)

It Happened in Bolivia. Dondeena Caldwell. A complete curriculum. Five lessons and all related activities and songs. $2.50 + S & H. Missions Education. (P)

Journey to Uzbekistan. Barbara Moody. Materials and activities to cover up to 5 lessons on the people and culture of Uzbekistan, written by one who was there. Write for cost and information to Barbara Moody, Caleb Project, 10 W. Dry Creek Circle, Littleton, CO 80120-4413 (see Resource Persons). (P,I)

Junior Missionary Retreat. Liz VonSeggen. Idea-filled packet provides all the information to plan a missions retreat for fifth and sixth graders. Juniors will focus on missions as they apply for passports, receive boarding passes, learn about culture shock, attend a hunger banquet and are challenged to listen to God's voice. Suggestions provide more than ample material to plan for a 24-hour "get-away." (RE-34) $10.00. From One Way Street.

Junior Teaching Resources. 13 lessons include three mission lessons, and can be used for worship time for Middler/Junior. Two of the missions lessons are adapted from the *Global Prayer Digest*, the only daily devotional focused on daily praying for the Unreached Peoples. Each lesson includes a teaching outline to give a 10-15 minute worship time lesson, ideally preparing children for the Sunday School Bible lesson. Call to ask for price. Scripture Press Publication..

Kinderclub Missions packets (Formerly World Christian Curriculum). Ele Parrott. Ten missions packets for Kindergarten and one for grades one through six. $6.50 each (S&H included), or all eleven for $71.50. Indicate desired packet(s), mailing address, and correct amount when ordering. From Highlands Community Church.

"God Loves...."

"The Philippines"	**"Me!"**
"Alaska (Natives)"	**"Thankful People"**
"Japan"	**"Germany"**
"Africa"	**"Israel"**
"Our Samaria"	**"South America"**

"KWAM!" ("Kid's With A Mission!"—1st–6th graders)

Knowing Christ Kit. For VBS, camp, 5-Day Club, Children's church, or Sunday School. Includes 5-lesson "Knowing Christ" flashcard story, 5-lesson "Devil-Kings and Cannibals" flashcard story, 5 visualized Bible verses, and "Knowing Christ" visualized song. $20.99. From CEF Press. (P,I)

Land Along the Nile. Dondeena Caldwell. A complete curriculum containing five lessons and all related activities and songs. $3.50 plus S & H. Missions Education. (P)

Let's Go To India. Elaine Meador. Part of Southern Baptist 1992 Foreign Mission Study. Tells stories about William Carey and present-day missionaries. Need to get Teaching Guide to teach it. For grades 1-3. #5438-92. $2.85. **Teaching Guide.** (WMU) #6297-86. $1.50. **Jesus Loves Me, Too** (Audiocassette for use with "Let's Go To India" and "Friends of India") for grades 1-6. Includes Indian music and Indian language version of familiar children's songs. 15 minutes. #4447-52. $4.95. From Baptist Book Store Mail Order Center.

Lost and Found Kit. For VBS, camp, 5-Day Club, Children's church, or Sunday School. Includes 5-lesson "Lost and Found" flashcard story, 5-lesson "Run, Ma, Run" flashcard mission story, 5 visualized Bible verses, and "No Longer Lost" visualized song. $20.99. From CEF Press. (P,I)

"Ly Huy's Escape." A Shining Star Club and/or Fisherkid's Club Missionary Lesson Plan book to accompany the missionary story, "Ly Huy's Escape" from Bible Visuals, Inc. Each lesson includes pre-session activities, story and song time, craft time, verse time, snack time, and closing activities. Order story from Bible Visuals and lesson plan book from Acorn Children's Publications. Specify Shining Club (Beginners) $6.50, or Fisherkid's Club (Primaries) $8.50. (P,I)

"Madugu." A Shining Star Club missionary lesson plan book to accompany the missionary story "Madugu" from Child Evangelism Fellowship Press. Each lesson includes pre-session activities, story and song time, craft time, verse time, snack time, and closing activities. Order story from CEF Press and lesson plan book from Acorn Children's Publications. $4.50. (P,I)

• **Mi Jun's Difficult Decision.** Dondeena Caldwell. A complete curriculum on Korea. Five lessons and all related activities and songs. $3.50 + S & H. Friendship Press. (I)

Mini-Missions Conference for Children. Dorothy Schultz. Using the classroom as their airplane cabin, children fly to any of five mission fields worldwide. Experience includes acquiring passports, immunization papers, airline tickets, etc. While on the field, they experience missionary life including foods, cultural distinctions, language barriers, etc. Seven units together would require approximately 25 hours class time. Books, in numerical order: *Getting Ready; Africa; Europe ; Asia; Pacific Region; Latin America; Going Home.* Complete Set of seven is $24.95, with individual options, $4.95 + $2.00 shipping. Detailed brochure available. R. C. Law and Co. (I,J)

Missionaries Tell About Jesus. A Tot Time Kit containing a leader's manual, resources, and one learning activities book. These three manuals can be ordered separately. Kit is $18.99. For pre-school and kindergarten. Accent Publications.

Missionary, The -- (Skituations). Steve and Cora Alley. Book contains all you will need for a series of ten lessons for children's worship, including drama skits, sermonettes, memory work, crafts, puzzles, games, coloring pages, and discussion questions. Written for performance by live adult actors, for children, but they are easily adaptable to use with puppets.

Includes double sets of scripts. See also Skits, Dramas. (DR-23) $20.00. One Way Street or Gannam/Kubat Publication. (I,J)

Missionary Stories About.... Flashcard series of "real-life" stories from around the world. Includes 8 sets of 13 stories, 52 flashcards per set. Stories alone are $5.95 per set. Pupils' activity handwork is $5.95 per set for five students. Leader's guide: $5.95. Randall house Publications. (P,I)

Missions Alive. Ivy Otto. Ten-lesson series that introduces children to the process of missionary application and appointment. Student packet includes activities, verses and crafts. One leader's book and one student packet FREE. May be photocopied. Conservative Baptist Foreign Mission Society. (I,J)

Motivating Missionary Ministries Packet for Your Church. Workable ways to integrate missions education throughout the entire church. Contains songs, memory verses, illustrated lessons, a few visuals; no pictures or stories. Also in Spanish. $8.75. Lakeland Bible Mission, Inc. (P,I,J)

Missions MatchFile Kits. Each MatchFile volume contains three learning topics and/or country topics with missions activities, games, stories, drama, Bible, and prayer activities. The activities range in length from 5-20 minutes, and are age graded. Easy to use. New self-contained study kits are available frequently. Published jointly by the Brotherhood Commission, SBC, and WMU/SBC, and available from Worldfriends Press. For grades 1-6.

Missions Study Packet ('95). Each year's packet is based on five themes: 1) Culture and Mission, 2) The Bible and Mission, 3) Christian Responsibility, 4) The Missionary,) The Mission Support Team. Each contains 8 to 12 large, full-color resource sheets, 24 masters of activity sheets, and a leader's guide. A new study packet is published each year. Each costs about $18.00. Call the number given for current packets, books and prices. From Children's Ministries/Division of S S Ministries, Nazarene Headquarters. (P,J,I)

Missions Units. Three-week units are developed by the Westlake Bible Church in Austin Texas. They are on Mexico, Kenya, Germany, Solomon Islands, China, and Romania. Available from Children's Ministries Department, Westlake Bible Church. (P)

Mustapha's Secret: A Muslim Boy's Search to Know God. Sandra Klaus. A 5-part Flashcard story tells of the courage and prayer it takes to convert from Islam to Christianity. helps children understand Muslims' need for salvation. 42 pp. (See Flashcards). $10.95, from Gospel Missionary Union. (P,I)

● **My Friends in India.** Jean Johnson. A complete curriculum. Five lessons and all related activities and songs. $2.50 + S & H. Missions Education. (P)

My Wonderful Lord Kit. For VBS, camp, 5-Day Club, children's church, or Sunday School. Includes 5-lesson "My Wonderful Lord" flashcard story, 5-lesson "Hudson Taylor" Mission flashcard story, 5 visualized Bible verses, and "Wonderful Counselor" visualized song. $20.99. From CEF Press. (P,I)

"Nathan of Israel." A Fisher Kid's Club Missionary Lesson Plan book to accompany the missionary story "Nathan Finds New Life in Jerusalem" from Bible Visuals, Incorporated. Each lesson includes pre-session activities, story and song time, craft time, verse time, snack time, and closing activities. Order story from Bible Visuals and lesson plan book from Acorn Children's Publications. $8.50. (P,I)

Neighbors Near and Far: Africans and Black Americans, Asians in Asia and North America, Hispanic North America and Latin America, and **Native People in North America.** Edna Kruger Dyck. All four contain resource sheets, 17 lesson/stories, project poster, people profiles, and map. Mission Education Kits of articles and artifacts may be ordered separately, though both courses are complete without them. Costs yet to be determined. General Conference Mennonite Church. (I)

"New Life for Iromo, A." A Shining Star Club Missionary Lesson Plan book to accompany the missionary story "A New Life for Iromo" from BCM Publications. Each lesson includes pre-session activities, story and song time, craft time, verse time, snack time, and closing activities. Order story from BCM Publications andlesson plan book from Acorn Children's Publications. $6.50. (P,I)

"No Darkness At All." A Shining Star Club Missionary Lesson Plan book to accompany the missionary story "No Darkness At All" from Bible Visuals, Inc. Each lesson includes pre-session activities, story and song time, craft time, verse time, snack time, and closing activities. Order story from Bible Visuals and lesson plan book from Acorn Children's Publications. $6.50. (P,I)

● **Our Amigos in America.** Dondeena Caldwell. A complete curriculum on Hispanics in America. Five lessons and all related activities and songs. $2.50 + S & H. Missions Education. (I)

Our Friend Kee Yazzie. Leroy Falling and Dondeena Caldwell. A complete curriculum on Navajos. Five lessons and all related activities and songs. $3.00 + S & H. Missions Education. (P)

Passport to Adventure. 13 lessons including: Will the Real Missionary Please Stand Up, Language Communicates God's Message, To Eat or Not to Eat. Item #137, $7.95 for teacher's guide. Available from Kids Can Make A Difference.

Pearl Makers. Six Stories About Children in the Philippines. Vilma May A. Fuentes. Learn about the problems of Filipino children in different parts of the country. Set amid the rich geographic and cultural variety of an island nation. $4.95 (For grades 1-6). Optional is the **Teachers' Guide to the Pearl Makers**, which makes it into a 6-session course. $5.95. From Friendship Press.

"Praying Hyde." A Shining Star Club and/or Fisherkid's Club Missionary Lesson Plan book to accompany the missionary story "Praying Hyde" from Bible Visuals, Inc. Tells the story of John Hyde. Each lesson includes pre-session activities, story and song time, craft time, verse time, snack time, and closing activities. Specify Shining Star Club (Beginners) $6.50, or Fisherkid's Club (Primaries)$8.50. Order story from Bible Visuals and lesson plan book from Acorn Children's Publications. (P,I)

"Ringu." A Shining Star Club and/or Fisherkid's Club Missionary Lesson Plan book to accompany the missionary story "Ringu of India's Forest" from Child Evangelism Fellowship Press. Each lesson includes pre-session activities, story and song time, craft time, verse time, snack time, and closing activities. Specify Shining Star Club (Beginners) $6.50, or Fisherkid's Club (Primaries) $8.50. Order story from CEF Press and lesson plan book from Acorn Children's Publications. (P,I)

"Run, Ma, Run." A Shining Star Club Missionary Lesson Plan book to accompany the missionary story "Run, Ma, Run" from Child Evangelism Fellowship Press. Tells the story of Mary Slessor. Each lesson includes pre-session activities, story and song time, craft time, verse time, snack time, and closing activities. Order story from CEF Press and lesson plan book from Acorn Children's Publications. $6.50. (P,I)

"Samuelito." A Shining Star Club Missionary Lesson Plan book to accompany the missionary story "A Miracle for Samuelito" from Bible Visuals, Inc. Each lesson includes pre-session activities, story and song time, craft time, verse time, snack time, and closing activities. Order story from Bible Visuals and lesson plan book from Acorn Children's Publications. $6.50. (P,I)

Secret Search, The. A complete curriculum about Taimoor, a Muslim boy in Pakistan. Includes a manual, containing 10 lessons of gripping stories, activities, craft instructions, worksheets, Kit includes large poster-size color photos and a wall-size map. Cost, $24.95 plus $2.00 shipping each. Available from Crossroads Publications Inc. (P, I)

Shining Star Club Missionary Lesson Plans (to accompany individual curricula). Acorn Children's Publications.

"So Send I You." History of missions in seven lessons. (See Visual Aids — Flannelgraph.)

"So Send I You." A Fisher Kid's ClubMissionary Lesson Plan book to accompany the missionary story "So Send I You" from BCM Publications (see above). Each lesson includes pre-session activities, story and song time, craft time, verse time, snack time, and closing activities. Order story from BCM Publications and lesson plan book from Acorn Children's Publications. $8.50. (P,I)

Strong In The Lord VBS Kit (1993). Design your VBS around the life of Daniel with the flashcard story, learning activities, review games and take-home challenges. Also includes director guide, two missionary hero stories, visualized missions song, missionary video, craft ideas and more. Complete kit, $89.99. From CEF Press. (P,I)

Surrounded By Headhunters. Sandra Klaus. Five flashcard story lessons about Frank and Marie Drown, missionaries to the Jivaro headhunters of Ecuador (see also Flashcards). Text also in Spanish, and one-color artwork. $10.95, from Gospel Missionary Union. (P,I)

Taiwan's Urban Working Peoples. Excellent multi-media kit. Includes four complete lessons, slides, colored pictures, map, overhead transparencies, notebook binder. $65.00. Available separately: a *People Groups of China* map ($5.00), and *Drawn to China*, an activity/coloring book (see Books). Institute of Chinese Studies. (Primarily for grades 4 to 6, but adaptable for adults.)

Through Latin America (NEW edition). A five-session course adaptable for Sunday School, Vacation Bible School, and day camp ministries. Includes visual aids, games, puzzles, slide show, and cassette tape. Send for brochure, or order complete at a cost of $40.00. Alice Cordova (see Resource Persons). (Oriented to fourth- and fifth-grade students.)

Trapped in Darkness. An exciting true story of two boys trapped behind the Iron Curtain. It includes a manual with an eight-episode story, 23 full-color poster-size pictures, master worksheets for both primary and junior children, cultural activities, and wall-size map of Romania. It is of the same fine quality as "Escape By Night." $24.95 plus $2.00 postage and handling. Crossroads Publications. (P,I)

Trip to the Land of the Rising Sun, A. Cheryl Barton. A complete curriculum. Five lessons and all related activities and songs. $3.00 + S & H. Missions Education. (I)

Welcome to India. Dondeena Caldwell. A complete curriculum. Five lessons and all related activies and songs. $2.50 + S & H. Missions Education. (I)

What Does A Missionary Do? #3. A series of 5 separate lessons to use for your Children's Conference, missionary time in VBS, or other Children's Ministries. Includes a missionary chorus, verse and visuals. $13.95, includes tax and shipping. From Lakeland Bible Mission, Inc. (I)

What in the World are Missions? Three five-lesson modular curricula, based on the principles that students learn best in small groups and through involvement. Includes full lesson plans for five one-hour sessions, activity center ideas and resource materials. Write for more information and prices, from SIM. Graded material, one book for each age level: 6-9, 10-12, youth to adult (indicate which).

Which Way To God? Five adaptable lessons to any kind of group includes active learning about: Where religions come from, Judaism, Islam, Eastern Religions, and Christianity. $9.95. Kids Can Make a Difference. (J)

Who is a Missionary? Barbara Campbell, author of *I Don't Want To Wait Until I'm Grown Up.* A set of 11 missions education lessons for elementary-aged children. Tried and tested with kids at Wheaton Bible Church, Wheaton, IL. Booklet of lessons, $12.00; package, including lessons, two video presentations, and flannelgraphs, $49.95. From ACMC.

"Witness-Servant-Chosen." #2. Lessons from Isaiah 43 for children's missionary conferences, Sunday School classes, VBS, or children's church. Includes song, memory verse and illustrated lesson. $11.29, includes tax and shipping. From Lakeland Bible Mission Inc. (I)

Won Gil's Secret Diary. Dondeena Caldwell. A complete curriculum from Korea. Five lessons and all related activities and songs. $3.50 + S & H. Friendship Press. (P)

Wordless Book Visualized Kit. For VBS, camp, 5-Day Club, children's church, or Sunday School. Includes 5-lesson "Wordless Book" flashcard story, 5-lesson "Ti-Fam" Mission flashcard story, 5 visualized Bible verses, and "G-O-S-P-E-L" visualized song. $20.99. From CEF Press. (P,I)

World Christian Curriculum (See Kinderclub)

WORLD FOCUS Curriculum Set. Bev Gundersen and Karen Robertson. Combines the *Unreached Peoples Booklets* and *Four Week Curriculum* by Karen , and the activities and some art work of Bev's former"*Winodow*" books, into a set. *Leader's Guide* must be purchased and used with any one or all of the set. Complete set, $40.00: Ask for new price list.

World Focus, Leader's Guide, all grades. $4.00.

World Focus, Tribal People Groups, Mexico, grade 1. $6.00.

World Focus, Chinese People Groups, China, grade 2. $6.00.

World Focus, Buddhist People Groups, Japan, grade 3. $6.00.

World Focus, Muslim People Groups, Indonesia, grade 4. $6.00.

World Focus, Hindu People Groups, India, grade 5. $6.00.

World Focus, World Christians (overview of all People Groups), grade 6. $6.00.

Worldtrek: 52 Missions Experieances for Children Grades 1-6. A leader's guide jointly produced by WMU and Brotherhood for use in children's programs. The 52 missions experiences are more like lessons, therefore resembling a curriculum which takes the child on a fun-filled journey, studying missions, hands-on experiences, stories and reinforcement activities, games, and Bible-based activities. Only 8 or 9 appear to focus on cross-cultural experiences. #6396-17. $15.95. From Baptist Book Store Center, or Worldfriends Press.

Yandicu: From Witch Doctor to Evangelist. Jeanette Windle with Jan Clements. Follow Yandicu Salinas, the Guarani Indian in Boliva, South America, who ws changed from witch doctor to evangelist after hearing the gospel from a GMU missionary. A true story, 5 lessons. Text only also in Spanish. $10.95. From Gospel Missionary Union. (P,I)

CURRICULA FOR YOUTH

Is This Missions Thing for Real? Features 10 solid Bible studies, three built-in outreach projects to help teenage young students learn missions by doing it, six exciting humorous video segments that grab students' interest, two handbooks with plans and listings of short-term missions projects, and more. High school ages. $49.95 plus shipping. From Harvest Publications.

Junior High Missions Curriculum. C. Dueck, G. Goulet, and B. Wiens. A team project developed in a Perspectives class, which teaches an awareness of God's global plan for unreached people groups. In four lessons it utilizes active class participation with plays, skits, games, Bible verse study, quizzes and prayer. $2.00. Children's Missions Resource Center.

Mission Trip! Notebook. Complete guide for putting together all the arragements for an overseas cross-cultural experience. Four lessons, 29 sample forms, articles for teens. Write for information to Beacon Hill Press.

2
BOOKS

For Children

• **Adventures in Africa.** Lorraine O. Schultz. A collection of eight exciting adventure stories, mostly from Mozambique. 44 pages, grade 2 and up, part of Understanding Christian Mission curriculum. Mark A. York, Editor. $3.00, Children's Ministries/Div of S S Ministries/Church of the Nazarene Headquarters.

Adventures of Tonko. Menzies. $2.10. SIM, USA. (P,I)

Ai-Chan's Secret. Irene Hope. $2.95. OMF BOOKS. (P,I)

Ainesworth Prowler, The (Debbie Newton Series). Peggy Albrecht. Illustrated. Order #658-6. $3.95, (I,J). Christian Literature Crusade.

All Paths Lead To Bethlehem. A unique blending of cultures with the Christmas story. From Kids Can Make A Difference.

Always a Friend. Jan Turrentine. From street gangs to the homeless, Mildred McWhorter ministers in Houston's inner city. #6210-70. $4.95. (New Hope) Baptist Book Store Center.

Amy Carmichael: Let the Little Children Come to Me. Lois Hadley Dick. 160 pages, tells how God used Amy to save the little children destined for a life in the temples. (6th-adult) from William Carey Library Publishers. MOP 433-2, $4.25, plus $2.00 shipping.

Ann H. Judson. E.R. Pitman. Biography of Mrs. Judson, missionary wife to "Judson of Burma." Order #601-2, $3.95. (I,J) Christian Literature Crusade.

Around the World With Logos. Tim Dowley. Illustrated history of the famous "floating bookshop." A great way to introduce children to world missions. Discount price, $3.95. From OM LIT. (P,I,J)

Attack in the Rye Grass. Dave and Neta Jackson. Story of Marcus and Narcissa Whitman. Part of the Trailblazer Series. A thrilling adventure story that introduces children (ages 8-12) to a missionary hero of the past. $4.99. Bethany House and Kids Can Make a Difference.

Bandit of Ashley Downs, The. Dave and Neta Jackson. Story of George Mueller. Part of the Trailblazer Series. A thrilling adventure story that introduces children (ages 8-12) to a missionary hero of the past. $4.99. Bethany House and Kids Can Make a Difference.

Bare Beautiful Feet, and Other Missionary Stories for Children. (see Stories) From Christian Publications.

Before the Moon Dies. Christa Weber. A boy in Thailand whose father is addicted to opium, and whose reputation as a thief may cost him his life. A missionary shows him how Jesus can change lives. 48 pages, illus. $2.95. See VIDEOS also. OMF BOOKS. (P,I)

Bobby In Japan. Mrs. Patricia Clark. A triumphant story of the son of missionaries who was a missionary for Jesus for only 8 short years before God took him home. 41 pages, grades 3 up. Price $2.00, from TEAM, Book Service.

Boy's War, A. David Mitchell. True story of the author's life in a Japanese concentration camp during World War II, and separation from his parents for six years. 6th-adult. 166 pages. $6.95, from OMF Books.

Broto. Adele Ellis. A story from Indonesia, 24 pages, illus. $2.95. William Carey Library and OMF BOOKS. (P)

Brown Eyes, Blue Eyes. Mary Frances McCullough. A good pre-school book, showing likenesses and differences in people, that God loves everyone. #6202-70. $3.95. Baptist Book Store Mail Order Center. (P)

By An Unfamiliar Path. Hope Marston. Book 13 in the Junior Jaffray Series follows missionaries David and Arlene Peters and their family to the mountains of Colombia and São Paulo, Brazil. $3.99. From Christian Publications. (P)

Catching Their Talk in a Box: The Life-Story of Joy Ridderhof, founder of Gospel Recordings. Betty M. Hockett. $4.95 plus 12% S & H. George Fox Press. (J,S,A)

Caudills, The: Courageous Missionaries. Tom McMinn. Missionaries in Cuba. 62 pages, illustrated. #4242-77. $5.95. Also available in Spanish ($2.95). Broadman Press. (I,J)

Child of Destiny. Connie Griffith. One in a series of three interesting books about a Hindu girl in South Africa. Published in England, but available from Africa Evangelical Fellowship. Call or write and ask for price. (I)

Christmas Around the World. An excellent resource book for planning a Christmas program. Learn how people in Mexico, Iran, China, Sweden, Iraq, Spain and Norway celebrate Christmas. From Kids Can Make A Difference.

City: Sights, Sounds, and Smells, The. Mary Frances McCullough. Parks, subways, tall buildings, church steeples—a trip to the city to help preschoolers learn that the people there need to know Jesus. #6286-42. $3.95. Baptist Mail Order Center. (P)

Colombian Jungle Escape. Autobiographical account of the ministry of Ed and Doreen Dulka and their children among the Carapana Indians of Colombia, including their capture by and escape from Marxist guerrillas. For children and teens, (175 pages). $5.00. Order from WEC International Media Dept.

Communicating the Christmas Story Cross-Culturally. Contains three lessons to help simulate a cross-cultural experience. From Kids Can Make A Difference.

Crusader for Christ. Jean Wilson. Biography of Billy Graham. Order #602-0. $3.95, (I,J). Christian Literature Crusade.

Culturgrams: Vol. 1 includes North & South America, West & East Europe. **Vol. 2** includes Middle East, Asia, Africa, Pacific. Each summarize in four pages unique customs, values, traditions, lifestyles of a country. Expanded and updated for 1994. $25.00 each Vol. Kids Can Make A Difference.

Curse of the Amulet, The (No. 4 in Asha's Adventures series). G.D. Lehmann & B. Norman. Fiction. For ages 10-14. Order #443-5. $4.95. Christian Literature Crusade.

Danger in the Blue Lagoon/Din Be Still. Hugh Steven. A "2-in-1 Book." Stories are about Mali in Micronesia and Din in Viet Nam. 64 pages. $2.95. Wycliffe Bible Translators. (I)

Danger on the Sunita. (No. 2 in Asha's Adventures series). G.D. Lehman. Fiction. For ages 9-12. Order #438-9. $4.95. Christian Literature Crusade.

Din Be Still/ Danger in the Blue Lagoon. Hugh Steven. (See above) Wycliffe Bible Translators.

Dr. Harms, the Helper. Linda S. Chandler. Story of Dr. David Harms, medical missionary in Honduras. $3.95. Baptist Book Store Mail Order Center. (P)

Doctor Who Never Gave Up, The. Carolyn Scott. Biography of Ida Scudder, missionary doctor in India. Order #607-1. $3.95, (I,J). Christian Literature Crusade.

Doña Maria & Friends. Marion Corley. Short illustrated stories from 20 years of missions work in Colombia. 250 pages. New Hope Publishing. (I,J,up)

Donald Orrs, The: Missionary Duet. Lee Hollaway. Music missionaries to Colombia, South America. #4242-83. $5.95. Also available in Spanish ($2.95). Broadman Press. (I,J)

Down a Winding Road: The Life-Story of Roscoe and Tina Knight, Missionaries to Bolivia, Peru, and Mexico City. Betty M. Hockett. $4.95 plus 12% S & H. George Fox Press. (J,S,A)

Drawn to China. Jim Ziervogel. A story, activity, coloring book. $3.95; quantity discounts available. Institute of Chinese Studies and OMF BOOKS. (P,I)

East Into Yesterday. Jeff Anderson Series #1. Alice Poyner. Jeff never dreamed that pushing a few buttons would catapult him into the adventure of his life. Lost in a foreign country and in another age, he finds himself face-to-face with nothing but Chinese people—and Hudson Taylor! $4.95 plus shipping. From OMF Books. (I,J)

East of the Misty Mountains. Jeff Anderson Series #2. Alice Poyner. Jeff visited Uncle Zeke's physics lab again and ended up clinging to a freezing mountain side. He was somewhere in time and space, but where—China, or Tibet, or Burma? He met J.O. Fraser, John and Isobel Kuhn and Orville Carlsons. $4.95 plus shipping. From OMF Books. (I,J)

East To the Shifting Sands. Jeff Anderson Series #3. Alice Poyner. Jeff and Shelley didn't expect any problems this time, when they pushed a few buttons in Jeff's Uncle's physics lab. But thieves stole the little "homer" device, stranding them in China again. Many exciting adventures followed, but they did meet Dr. Kao, Mildred Cable and Eva and Francesca French. $4.95 plus shipping. From OMF Books. (I,J)

Ed Taylor: Father of Migrant Missions. Lou Heath. Home missionary to migrant workers. #4242-78. $5.95. Broadman Press. (P,I)

Edge of Conflict. Barbara Hibschman. Book 8 of the Junior Jaffray Collection of Missionary Stories. Tells the exciting story of the adventures of Harry and Miriam Taylor, missionaries to Cambodia. $3.99. Christian Publications. (P)

Escape From the Slave Traders—David Livingstone. Dave and Neta Jackson. Part of the Trailblazer Series. A thrilling adventure story that introduces children (ages 8-12) to a missionary hero of the past. $4.99. Bethany House and Kids Can Make a Difference.

Eric Liddell. Catherine Swift. True story of the famous runner and hero of the film, "Chariots of Fire," and returned as a missionary to China. 6th-adult. 176 pages. $3.99, from Bethany House.

Escape From the Darkness. Connie Griffith. One in a series of three books, about a Hindu girl in South Africa. From Africa Evangelical Fellowship. (I)

Ethnic Pride. Greta Lipson. This secular book identifies 103 ethnic groups in America. Fascinating, cultural information, 170 activities and personal research sheets help children enrich their ethnic pride; for school and home school, grades 4-9. 152 pages. $11.95. From Universal Four.

"Family In" Series, The. See how your family is similar or different to Muslim in these countries: **Oman, Morocco, Egypt, Pakistan, India, Sudan, Peru, Australia, Japan,** .... Nineteen books in all. All are 32 pages long, hard-bound, with large color photos on every page. $8.95 each from Lerner Publications. Indicate which country when ordering. Item #191 when ordering from Kids Can Make A Difference. (P,I)

Finley and Julia Graham: Missionary Partners. Johnnie Human. Mission work in Bible-lands (Middle East). #4243-27. $5.95. Broadman Press. (I,J)

Flight from Death. V. Ben Kendrick. Dynamic missionary stories from Africa to share with children or use as illustrations. $4.95. Baptist Mid-Missions Women's Department. (I,J)

Flight of the Fugitives—Gladys Aylward. Dave and Neta Jackson. Part of the Trailblazer Series. A thrilling adventure story that introduces children (ages 8-12) to a missionary hero of the past. Tells how Gladys faced the tragedies of war; and how she worked to save nearly a hundred orphans in China, from lives of terror and abandonment. $4.99. Bethany House and Kids Can Make a Difference.

Friend of the Chiefs. Iris Clinton. Biography of Robert Moffat, missionary in Southern Africa. Order #608-X. $3.95, (I,J). Christian Literature Crusade.

•**Friends Around the World Series.** Each book helps elementary-age students explore the culture, setting and daily lives of children in other areas of the world. Includes stories, games, puzzles and other activities. From Augsburg Fortress Press. (P,I):

Friends in Asia. $3.50.

Friends in Africa: A World Mission Activity Book. $3.50.

Friends in Latin America. (Cost unknown)

From Arapesh to Zuni. Karen Lewis. An easy-to-read story of Bibleless peoples, one group for each letter of the alphabet. Beautiful full-color pictures. $4.00 (discount) from William Carey Library, and from Wycliffe.

From Here to There and Back Again: The Life-Story of Dr. Charles DeVol, Missionary to China and Taiwan. Betty M. Hockett. $4.95 plus 12% S & H. George Fox Press. (J,S,A)

From Slave Boy to Bishop. John Milsome. Biography of Samuel Adjai Crowther, born in West Africa, who became the first black Anglican bishop. Order #600-4. $3.95, (I,J). Christian Literature Crusade.

George Lozuks, The: Doers of the Word. Roberta Ryan. Mission work in Venezuela and Ecuador. #4242-93. $5.95. Broadman Press. (I,J)

God's Madcap. Nancy Robbins. Biography of Amy Carmichael, founder of Dohnavur Fellowship in India. Order #604-7. $3.95, (I,J). Christian Literature Crusade.

Gods Must Be Angry, The. Sheila Miller and Ian Murray. Brodit loved to play at his home in Thailand, then disaster struck—his stick knocked the head off the Happy Idol. Brodit is now a pastor. 33pp. OMF 293-X, $2.50 (discount), from William Carey Library. (P,I)

Golden Foot. J.R. Batten. Biography of Adoniram and Ann Judson, courageous missionaries to Burma. Order #628-4. $3.95, (I,J). Christian Literature Crusade.

Granny Han's Breakfast. S. Groves. $2.95. OMF BOOKS and William Carey Library. (P,I)

Happiness Under the Indian Trees: The Life-Story of Catherine Cattell, Missionary to India and Taiwan. Betty M. Hockett. $4.95 plus 12% S & H. George Fox Press. (J,S,A)

Happy Day for Ramona, A, and Other Missionary Stories for Children. (see Stories). Christian Publications.

Harley Shields, The: Alaskan Missionaries. Kathryn W. Kizer. Missionaries to Alaska. #4242-85. $5.95. Broadman Press. (P,I)

Hattie Gardner: Determined Adventurer. Judy Latham. Missionary to Nigeria. #4242-80. $5.95. Broadman Press. (I,J)

Heart for Imbabura, A. BarbaraHibschman. Book 6 ofthe Junior Jaffray Collection of Missionary Stories. Tells the exciting story of the adventures of Evelyn Rychner, missionary among the Indians in Ecuador, South America. $3.99. Christian Publications. (P)

Heroine of Newgate, The. John Milsome. Biography of Elizabeth Fry, who worked among women prisoners in London and Australia. Order #633-0. $3.95, (I,J). Christian Literature Crusade.

Hidden Jewel, The—Amy Carmichael. Dave and Neta Jackson. Part of the Trailblazer Series. A thrilling adventure story that introduces children (ages 8-12) to a missionary hero of the past. $4.99. Bethany House and Kids Can Make a Difference.

House Beyond Congo Cross, The (Dibbie Newton Series). Peggy Albrecht. Illustrated. Order #651-9. $3.95. (I,J) Christian Literature Crusade.

Hudson Taylor, Trusting God. Stocker. $3.95. Overseas Missionary Fellowship.

I Heard Good News Today. Cornelia Lehn. 148 pages, hardcover. $12.95, plus S & H. Facinating stories of early missionaries to Germany. Faith and Life Press. (All children).

I Want To Be a Missionary. From **Missionary—That's Me Series**. Barbara Hibschman. A very easy to read 24 page book that illustrates go, show, and tell, and what it would be like to be missionaries when they grow up. $4.99. Christian Publications. (P)

Ian and the Gigantic Leafy Obstacle. Sheila Miller. Tells about a missionary's travels and travails in Thailand from his land rover's point of view. 32 pages. Also on video. $2.95. OMF BOOKS. (P,I)

Imprisoned in the Golden City—Adoniram Judson. Dave and Neta Jackson. Part of the Trailblazer Series. A thrilling adventure story that introduces children (ages 8-12) to a missionary hero of the past. $4.99. Bethany House and Kids Can Make a Difference.

It Was Always Africa. Pam Brown. Follow Josephine Scaggs' journey from her youth in Oklahoma to womanhood in the depths of the African forest. $4.95. Baptist Book Store Mail Order Center. (J,S)

Jim Elliot, Missionary to the Rain Forest. Sue Shaw. Color pictures illustrate the victorious story of this modern day martyr. Discount price, $3.50. From OM LIT. (P,I,J)

John Allen Moores, The: Good News in War and Peace. Mary and Trent Butler. Missionaries to Europe. #4242-95. $5.95. Broadman Press. (I,J)

John and Julie Go to Japan. Carol Perkins. The children of an American family living in Japan meet the Japanese children living next door. Contains activities and teaching guide. Foreign Mission Board, Southern Baptist Convention. (P)

Joy to the World. Christmas celebrations and craft activities from 12 different countries. $10.70. Kids Can Make A Difference.

Kazuko's Family. Chris Shelby. Lifestyles and Baptist mission work in Japan. Foreign Mission Board, Southern Baptist Convention. (I)

Keeping Them All In Stitches. Betty M. Hockett. One of the "Life-Story From Missions" series. Story of Geraldine Custer, missionary to Burundi, Africa. Available from George Fox Press. $4.95 pus 12% shipping. (J,I)

Kim and Ting. Miriam Dunn. Kim excaped from Communist China after the Red Guards visited his village. In Hong Kong he made friends with Ting and the two boys had some very exciting adventures. $3.95. OMF BOOKS , also from William Carey Library) (I)

Knight of the Snows. R.G. Martin. Biography of Wilfred Grenfell, missionary in Labrador. Order #609-8. $3.95, (I,J). Christian Literature Crusade.

Kwanzaa. Tells of an African-American Christmas holiday. From Kids Can Make A Difference.

Lady of Courage: The Story of Lottie Moon. Ann Kilner Hughes. Biography of a missionary to China. 62 pages, ilustrated. New Hope Publishing/WMU. (J)

Lloyd Corder, Traveller for God. E. Chamberlain. Missionary to the Spanish-speaking. #4242-84. $5.95. Broadman Press. (I,J)

Let My People Go. Barbara Hibschman. Book 1 of the Junior Jaffray Collection of Missionary Stories. Tells the story of Robert Jaffray, pioneer missionary to China. $3.99. Christian Publications. (P)

Loompy—Mission Dog. Sheila Groves. True story of a dog who lives at the OMF German hostel in Singapore with German-speaking MKs (missionary kids). $2.95. OMF BOOKS. (P)

Making Missions Meaningful. Lila Bishop and Douglas Livingston. Resource book for Pioneer Clubs containing many stories and missionary activities for grades 1-8. $10.00 to members of Pioneer Clubs, and $15.00 plus shipping to non-members. (see Leader's section.) Pioneer Ministries.

Maki's Busy Week. Linda Hinchliffe. Maki's home in a Manobo tribal village on the island of Mindanao, Southern Philippines is very different from Western houses. He helps do the washing in the river, and even takes his pig to church. $2.95. OMF BOOKS and William Carey Library. (P,I)

Man Who Would Not Hate, The. Based on the life of Festo Kievngere in Uganda. Item #220, $4.99. From Kids Can Make A Difference.

Matthew's Dad is a Missionary. Kathy Strawn. The story of Dr. William Swan, missionary doctor in Macao. $2.95. Baptist Book Store Mail Order Center. (P)

Meet the Missionary. Mark Weinrich. Part of the **Missionary—That's Me Series**. Brightly colored decorations, a parade and even a special birthday cake--no wonder the children are excited about missionary conference! But most important, they learn what being a missionary is all about. $4.99. From Christian Publications. (P)

Millionaire for God. John Erskine. True story of C.T. Studd who gave away his fortune and became a missionary in China, India, and Africa (children and teens). 95 Pages. $4.00. From CLC. (I,J)

Missing Missionary, The. Mark Weinrich. Part of the **Missionary—That's Me Series**. The Missionary Detective Club has to find out during the missionary conference where the missing missionary is. Where will the children look? $4.99. From Christian Publications. (P)

Mission Adventures in Many Lands. J. Lawrence Driskill. Includes 53 mission stories from various countries—many from Japan. A read-to-me book, or 4th grade up reading. From William Carey Library. Published originally by Hope Publishing House, paperback, 212 pages. $10.00 discount plus $2.00 handling, from William Carey Library Publishers.

Mission Stories For Young Children. Barbara Oliver. (see Stories for description) New Hope.

Mission Stories From Around the World. J. Lawrence Driskill. Contains 44 mission stories from 16 different countries. A read-to-me book for small children, or 4th grade up reading. $10.00 (discount) from William Carey Library.

Missionary That's Right. Mark Weinrich. Part of the **Missionary—That's Me Series.** Jeremy is teased at school for wanting to be a missionary, so Mom takes him on a little trip to show how important helping people know Jesus really is. $4.99. From Christian Publications. (P)

Mud on Their Wheels, the Story of Vern and Lois Ellis in Navajo Land. Betty Hockett. $4.95 plus 12 percent shipping. George Fox Press. (J)

My Book About Hudson. S. Miller. Soft cover, $2.95, hard cover, $5.95. OMF BOOKS also from William Carey Library, $2.60 (discount). (P)

Mystery of the Scar. Connie Griffith. One in a series of three books, about a Hindu girl in South Africa. From Africa Evangelical Fellowship. (I)

Never Hide a Hyena in a Sack. Penny. $4.00. New 1994 edition. SIM, USA. (P,I)

New Toes for Tia. Larry Dinkins. $2.95. OMF BOOKS. (P)

Nid's Exciting Day. Mary Gurtler. $2.95. OMF BOOKS and William Carey Library, $2.50 (discount). (P,I)

Night of the Long Knives. Hugh Steven. Anthology of stories about children from Central and South America, Africa, and Australia. 118 pages. $2.98. Wycliffe Bible Translators. (I)

No Sacrifice Too Great. Barbara Hibschman. Book 7 in the Junior Jaffray Collection of Missionary Stories. Tells the story of missionary life—sacrifice and rewards, excitement and intrigue. About Ernest and Ruth Presswood in Borneo. $3.99. Christian Publications. (P)

No Time Out. Betty M. Hockett. One of the **"Life-Story From Mission"** series by the same author. George and Dorothy Thomas discover that following God's call can be truly adventurous as they meet snakes and lions in Burundi and Rwanda, Africa, and find new friends among the Navajo Indians in the Arizona desert. $4.95 plus 12% shipping. From George Fox Press. (I,J)

Nothing Daunted. Gloria Repp. Story of Isobel Kuhn. In her despair she began a search to know God that led her to the adventurous life of a missionary in the wilderness of southwest China. 167 pages. $5.95. From God's World Publications. (J and Up)

On Call. Book 3 in the Junior Jaffray Collection of Missionary Stories. Tells the exciting story of the adventures of David Thompson, MD, missionary doctor in Gabon, West Africa. $3.99. Christian Publications. (P)

On the Trail of a Spy (No. 1 in Asha's Adventures). G.D. Lehmann. Fiction. For ages 8-11. Order #437-0. $4.95. Christian Literature Crusade.

One Shall Chase a Thousand. Barbara Hibschman. Book 9 of the Junior Jaffray Collection of Missionary Stories. Tells the exciting story of the adventures of Mabel Francis, missionary to Japan. $3.99. Christian Publications. (P)

Outside Doctor On Call. Betty M. Hockett. Fascinating boigraphy of Dr. Ezra DeVol, and his nurse/wife Frances. With prayer they faced success and failure, war and peace, and medical emergencies in China, India, Nepal and the U.S. $4.95 plus 12 percent shipping. George Fox Press. (J)

Oz and Mary Quick: Taiwan Teammates. W. McElrath. Missionaries to Taiwan. #4242-87. $5.95. Broadman Press. (I,J)

Pattersons, The: Missionary Publishers. Janet Hoffman. Missionaries to Mexico. #4242-88. $5.95. Broadman Press. (I,J)

People Book. Peter Spier. A classic illustrated book about how people from various cultures are different and alike. Giant size—17'x22'. $21.00. Kids Can Make A Difference.

Pink and Green Church, The, and Other Missionary Stories for Children. (see Stories) From Christian Publications.

Please Leave Your Shoes at the Door. Barbara Hibschman. Book 5 in the Junior Jaffray Collection of Missionary Stories. The exciting story of the adventures of Corrine and Elmer Sahlberg, missionaries to Thailand. $3.99. Christian Publications. (P)

Potato Story, The, and Other Missionary Stories for Children. (see Stories) Unique and miraculous true stories from Mali, Peru, Navajoland, China, Cote d'Ivoire, Vietnam, Argentina, India and Zaire. Published by Christian Publications; also available from Kids Can Make A Difference, Item #133, $3.99.

Prophet of the Pacific. Margaret Kabell. Biography of John G. Paton, missionary from Scotland to the remote islands of the New Hebrides. Order #619-5. $3.95 (I,J). Christian Literature Crusade.

Question of Yams, A. Kuri's father plants yams without praying to the spirits because Father declares "God is mighty." Story from Papua New Guinea. Item #165, $5.95. From Kids Can Make A Difference.

Rat-Catcher's Son, The. Carolyn London. In their home in Nigeria, Sunday and her young brother, Little Lion, listen eagerly to their wise old grandfather, Baba, tell them stories. Each of the nine stories speaks to them about some situation which they face in daily life. $4.20. SIM, USA. (P,I)

Red Gang, The (No. 3 in Asha's Adventures series). G.D. Lehmann & B. Norman. Fiction. For ages 9-13. Order # 439-7. $4.95. Christian Literature Crusade.

Rick-a-Chee Series: Big Trouble for Rick-a-Chee; Rick-a-Chee and the Littlest Puppy; Rick-a-Chee and the Naughty Monkeys; Rick-a-Chee and the Runaway Kobos; Rick-a-Chee and the Sky-Blue Cap; Rick-a-Chee Takes a Journey. A series of stories on the life of an African boy. Ready-to-color illustrations. $2.85 each, $17.25 for all six. Also available on video. From SIM, USA. (P)

Saint in the Slums. Cyril Davey. Biography of Toyohiko Kagawa, who went to live in the slums of Tokyo bacause he wanted to be like Christ. Order #620-9. $3.95, (I,J). Christian Literature Crusade.

Saved by Fire (No. 5 in Asha's Adventures series). G.D. Lehmann. Fiction. For ages 10-15. Order #441-9. $4.95. Christian Literature Crusade.

Secret of the Forest Hut. Menzies. $3.75. SIM, USA. (P,I)

Secret of the Old House, The (Debbie Newton Series). Peggy Albrecht. Illustrated. Order #6305. $3.95, (I,J). Christian Literature Crusade.

Shanghaied to China--Hudson Taylor. Dave and Neta Jackson. Part of the Trailblazer Series. A thrilling adventure story that introduces children (ages 8-12) to a missionary hero of the past. $4.99. Bethany House and Kids Can Make a Difference.

Shoemakers, The: God's Helpers. Elsie Rives. Mission work in Latin America. #4243-28. $5.95. Broadman Press. (P,I)

Shoes On, Shoes Off. Catherine H. Compher. Preschool storybook about Japanese children by an adult MK who grew up in Japan. #6360-76. $6.95. Baptist Book Order Center.

Snake Stories from Africa. Bingham. Illustrated. $4.00. Cassette available. SIM, USA. (P,I)

South Seas Sailor. Cecil Northcott. Biography of John Williams, fearless missionary to the South Pacific islands. Order #622-5. $3.95, (I,J). Christian Literature Crusade.

Spice Islands Mystery. Alice Poynor. A mystery adventure about Alan Carter's visit to Indonesia, which takes a mysterious twist when he enters the airport. A theft and a series of strange incidents lead to a whole lot more than sightseeing—perhaps a lot of trouble. $3.95. OMF BOOKS. (I,J)

Star Over Gobi. Cecil Northcott. Biography of Mildred Cable's missionary adventures across the Gobi desert in Asia. Order #624-1. $3.95, (I,J). Christian Literature Crusade.

Stories from Africa. Various authors. Illustrated. $4.50. Cassette available. SIM, USA. (P,I)

Tales of Persia. William McElwee Miller. 23 chapters of stories with setting in Iran and much background information about Islam. Published by Presbyterian and Reformed Publishing Co., but available from Iranian Christians International Inc. (all age children)

Then and Now: The CIS States. A unique and timely series. Great for background information for anyone working with the Co-Mission or Advance. States available: **Armenia, Azerbaijan, Belarus, Estonia, Georgia, Kazakhstan, Latvia, Lithuania, Moldova, Rus-**

sia,Tajikistan, Turkmenistan, Ukraine, Uzbekistan. $15.95 for 1, $12.95 for 2 or more. Kids Can Make A Difference. (J) (All)

To China and Back. Grace B. Cutts. Book 4 of the Junior Jaffray Collection of Missionary Stories. This is the exciting story of the adventures of Anthony and Evelyn Bollback, missionaries to China. $3.99. Christian Publications. (P,I)

To Vietnam With Love. Hope Marston. Book 12 of the Junior Jaffray Collection of Missionary Stories. Follows Charlie and EG Long and their four children to Vietnam during the war. $3.99. From Christian Publications. (P)

Toby's Story. $12.00. Kids Can Make A Difference. (P)

Trial by Poison—Mary Slessor. Dave and Neta Jackson. Part of the Trailblazer Series. A thrilling adventure story that introduces children (ages 8-12) to a missionary hero of the past. $4.99. Bethany House and Kids Can Make a Difference.

Two Dreams and a Promise: The Story of William and Frances Skinner of Paraguay. $4.25. Baptist Book Store Mail Order Center.

Two Nichols, The: Spent for Missions. Jester Summers. Missionaries in China and Indonesia. #4242-79. $5.95. Broadman Press. (I,J)

Vena Aguillard: Woman of Faith. Marsha Barret. Missionary to the French-speaking people of Louisiana. #4242-81. $5.95. Broadman Press. (I,J)

Virginia Wingo: Teacher and Friend. Barbara Massey. Missionary to Italy. #4242-82. $5.95. Broadman Press. (P,I)

Visiting in the Global Village, Volume 1 (El Salvador, Tanzania, Japan). Each 24-page book includes eight pages of full color scenes from featured countries. $1.95 Available from Augsburg Fortress. Write for catalog. Publishers in other locations also.

Visiting in the Global Village, Volume 2 (Indonesia, Cameroon, Brazil) $1.95. Same description and publisher as above.

Visiting in the Global Village, Volume 3 (India, Peru, Madagascar) $1.95. Same description and publisher as above.

Waiting Missionary, The. David Fessenden. Part of the **Missionary—That's Me Series.** Jasmine and her brother find out that Pastor Luis has heard God's call to be a missionary. But he has to wait! There's a lot of work to get ready to go—including eating your vegetables! $4.99. From Christian Publications. (P)

Weak Thing in Moni Land. Grace B. Cutts. Book 2 in the Junior Jaffray Collection of Missionary Stories. Tells the exciting story of the adventures of Bill and Gracie Cutts, missionaries to the Moni Tribe in Irian Jaya. $3.99. Christian Publications. (P)

What Will Tomorrow Bring? The Life-Story of Ralph and Esther Choate, missionaries to Burundi, Africa. Betty M. Hockett. $4.95 plus 12% S & H. George Fox Press. (J,S,A)

When I Grow Up, I Can Go Anywhere for Jesus. Terry Whalin. Hardback, colorful blend of photos, illustration, and text to whet children's imaginations for all the things they might do when they grow up. Helps them to see they can serve Jesus anywhere in the world (ages 4–7). Hardcover. $8.49. Available in Christian bookstores, or order from William Carey Library Publishers, Chariot/David C. Cook Publications, or Wycliff. (P,I)

Whistling Bombs and Bumpy Trains, the Story of Anna Nixon in the Philippines and India. Betty Hockett. $4.95 plus 12 percent shipping. George Fox Press.

White Queen; Mary Slessor. Donald McFarlan. Scottish missionary to the Afriacan tribes in Calabar. Order #632-2.$3.95, (I,J). Christian Literature Crusade.

Who is a Missionary? A glimpse into the life of a foreign missionary. Illustrated to appeal to preschoolers. $3.95. Baptist Book Store Mail Order Center. (P)

With Daring Faith: A Biography of Amy Carmichael. Unafraid of criticism, Amy Carmichael revealed to the Western world the spiritual bondage of India as well as the suffering of thousands under Hinduism. 187 pages. $5.95, from God's World Publications. (J)

Wizard of the Great Lake. Donald McFarland. Biography of Alexander Mackay as he explored around Lake Victoria and Uganda to bring the Gospel to people in Africa. Order # 631-4. $3.95, (I,J). Christian Literature Crusade.

Yes Lord! What NOW? Su Cochran. A 25-page 3-color illustrated book designed to: REIN-FORCE the 8-12 year old's commitment to life-time involvement in missions; DIRECT the young "goer" or "sender" to immediate missions involvement in his local church; IN-STRUCT the yielded young person in steps of preparation which will lead to fulfillment of God's plan for his life. $1.50 each, or missionary discount on orders of 10 or more, 25%. From BCM Youth Ministries, P.O. Box 268, Annville, PA 17003-0268. Also see BCM Publications.

You Can be a Musician and a Missionary, Too. Renee Kent. Meet five "real live" missionaries who share God's love through music. $2.95. Baptist Book Store Mail Order Center. (I)

You Can Change the World. Jill Johnstone. Children's edition of **Operation World** is in color-ful two-page spread, about countries and cultures, placed in alphabetical order. Illustra-tions depict 26 countries and 26 people groups, their locations, their unique traits, and their needs. Prayer suggestions for a week are given, so the book can be used, one section a week, for a year. Elementary and up. Hardcover, $10.50 discount from William Carey Library Publishers.

Young Man in a Hurry. Iris Clinton. Biography of William Carey, pioneer of modern missions in India. Order #630-6. $3.95, (I,J). Christian Literature Crusade.

For Leaders

Amy Carmichael. Kathleen White. The Irish missionary to India whose life and writings con-tinue to touch the world. A poet, hymnwriter and author, she founded Dohnavur Fellow-ship in India. (6th-adult) 126 pages. $4.99, from Bethany House.

Annotated Bibliography of Resources for Contemporary Missions Education and Cultural Awareness, The. Laurie Eve Loftin, Missions Education Specialist. The NEW (March 31, 1995) booklet contains over 260 entries, 150 of which are new for 1995-96, with contact in-formation for 75 key sources. Lists sources, materials, and listings for both children and adults. For a copy, send a self-addressed, 9"x12" envelope, stamped and marked for first-or third-class postage (sufficient for 4 oz. per copy). Contact: Joyce L. Gibson, Editorial Di-rector, PO Box 632, Glen Ellyn IL 60138 USA.

Any Old Time Book No 5. Paul Borthwick. 80 pp. Manual containing 16 missions youth programs, especially for Junior and Senior High. Victor/SP Publications. (J,S,A)

Bibles and New Testaments, in many Internationl languages. Prices vary. Request Catalog. Order must be with credit card. International Bible Society.

Carousel of Countries, A. Mary Kinney Branson. A resource book for leaders containing activities. (See Activities) From New Hope Publishing.

Catalog/Kids Can Make a Difference. Bi-annual catalog of mission resources to use with children in school, home and church. One stop shopping. FREE. Kids Can Make A Difference (Jan Bell).

Chalkboard, The. Educational Supplies Catalog listing such items as Bulletin Boards, Decorations, Flash Cards, Games, Geography Activity Books, Maps (world and country), Ornaments, Story Cards, and many more items adaptable as missions education resources. Request Catalog. From The Chalkboard.

God's 4 Kids Book Club. "The all-Christian book club for kids." Monthly, grade-specific offers of "books and things" with "Christian morals, Christian values and Christian teaching according to the Word of God." Mission books often included. God's 4 Kids.

Great Missionaries in a Great Work: Leader's Guide for Junior Age Missionary Programs. Evelyn Mangham. 84 pp. Christian Publications. (I)

Home School Guide to World Missions, The. Ann Dunagan. A listing of available missions resources appropriate for home schooling includes: information books on world missions (for all ages), Mission stories of children and people from around the world, missionary biographies, videos, teaching and music tapes, tracts, foreign language instruction, examples of world atlases, globes, posters and maps, international rubber stamps, stickers, and international craft products, puzzles, toys and games, examples of children's Bible storybooks and other appropriate teaching supplies. Also includes a description and evaluation of each major item, including a photograph, current prices, and address, phone number, and publisher/distributor. Write Ann Dunagan (See Resource Persons).

How We Teach Missions in the Home. A leaflet for parents who would like help involving their family in missions. 25 cents. Baptist Book Store Mail Order Center.

I Don't Want To Wait Until I'm Grown Up. Barbara Campbell. Excellent 88-page children's Mission Education Curriculum Development Guide and teaching manual is published by ACMC. Includes resource lists and specific chapters for early childhood, second- to third-graders, and fourth- through sixth-graders, and suggested lesson plan instructions for designing the curriculum, why, what, and how to plan, and much more. Cost: Members $9.95; non-members $14.95, plus shipping. From ACMC.

Junior High Curriculum. C. Dueck and B. Wiens. 18 pp. Emphasizes "Hidden Peoples." $2.00. Children's Missions Resource Center. (J)

Kids for the World: A Guidebook to Children's Mission Resources. Gerry Dueck. $12.95. William Carey Library. (All ages.)

Making Missions Meaningful. Resource book for Pioneer Clubs ontaining many stories, Bible lessons, games, snacks, missionary lessons, and missionary activitiy pages for grades 1-8. 64 pages, illustrated. $15.00 for non-members and $10.00 for members. Payment must accompany all orders under $10.00. No phone orders under $20.00. Pioneer Ministries.

Mission Frontiers Mission Resource Catalog. The William Carey Library Publishers Catalog, listing all the best in ALL missions materials for all ages, including maps, videos, and study materials. Send for FREE copy from Mission Frontiers, the bulletin of the U.S. Center for World Mission, Circulation Dept.

Missionary Program Builder. Poems, songs recitations, and skits help present the missionary's goals and needs. Much of this booklet is written specifically to be performed by, or to include children. (RE-39) $3.95. From One Way Street. (P,J)

Missions Alive. Charlie Warren. A text and study guide book for Junior and Senior High youth, helping them study the lives of five past, present, and future missionaries. #51344. Cost unknown. Baptist Book Store (or call 1-800-458-BSSB)

Missions Alive. David A. Howard. Experiential games and activities for teens to emphasize a global view of missions and ministry to other cultures. $5.95. World Changers Resources.

Missions Games and Activities For Youth. Practical, helpful, and flexible resources for youth leaders, to plan games, music, drama, and more. $3.95. World Changers Resources.

Missions Ideas. 100 pages of songs, giving projects, stories, things to make and do, and much more to encourage children to be involved in worldwide missions. For all ages. Order item #0005, cost $12.00. Order from Sacred Literature Ministries. (Also see Activities)

Missions Made Fun For Kids. Elizabeth Whitney Crisci. Build missions-minded childen as each page presents missionary truth and challenges students with personal responsibility, using creative ideas to involve children in missions. 128 pages. All ages of children. $7.95. Accent Publications. Also available from William Carey Library.

Missions Material For Kids. By Margaret Muir. A 40-page resource manual. Order from Margaret Muir, Wycliffe Bible Translators, South Central Regional Office, 1 South 210 Summit Ave., Oakbrook Terrace, IL 60181. (708) 495-1307.

Motivating Children for Missions. Jackie Roberts. A 30-page collection of reprinted articles, suggestions, and resources; especially strong on missions in the home. Jackie Roberts. (A)

Operation World (5th Edition). Patrick Johnstone. This absolutely essential, most informative, easy-to-use "prayer guide for the nations" opens up factual information about every country of the world to see what God has been doing there. Designed to equip you to pray for the countries and peoples of the world. A MUST for every teacher of children. 608 pages, illustrated. $14.99 (retail); $9.75 (discount), plus $2.00 shipping. From William Carey Library Publishers or WEC Literature–Operation World.

Peace Child. Don Richardson. This cliff-hanging, true account is not only a masterpiece of story-telling but presents a startling new approach—the redemptive analogy—that is truly revolutionary for all pioneer missionary work. 288 pages. RGL415-9, $6.50(disc.). From William Carey Library. Good for all ages. (See also Videos)

Reach Around the World. 52 missions activities for youth. (see Activities for description)

Savage, My Kinsman, The. Elizabeth Elliott. Contains many pictures. Stories can be adapted for children. Paperback, $6.95. Christian Publications. (J,I,A)

Youth and Missions: Expanding Your Students' World View. Paul Borthwick. A practical handbook of how to move teenagers to world missions. Includes principles, guidelines, and examples. 160 pp. $6.95. Victor/SP Publications. (S,A)

What About the Children? Esther Ilnisky. Instruction book containing informative, challenging, sound Biblical principles for leading children to pray through the 10/40 Window. $4.00. From Esther Network International.

WORM (World Outreach Resource Material). Sandra Kimber. 100-page missions resource catalog for children and youth. Especially helpful to those in the U.K. Write to Sandra Kimber, EMA Youth Ministries, P.O. Box 18, Teddington, Middx TW11 8UX, ENGLAND.

3
STORIES

Bare, Beautiful Feet, and Other Missionary Stories for Children. Contains nine real-life, illustrated missionary stories from around the world. 52 pages. $3.99. From Christian Publications. (P,I)

Brazil Nut, The. Contributed by Kathy Yamada. An object lesson illustrating how the Brazil Nut actually grows inside two large hard shells. Write to Children's Missions Resource Center for FREE copy. (P,I)

Children's Mission Sermons. See Curricula.

Children's Mission Stories. From Mission to the World (Presbyterian Church in America).

Chinese Mayor, The. Author Unknown. A story illustrating how the Chinese Mayor became little in his own sight, but big in God's sight after he accepted Jesus Christ. Send for story and visual-aid pattern (FREE) from Children's Missions Resource Center. (P,I)

Choices and Other Stories From the Caribbean. Seven captivating stories describe turning points in the lives of children in Cuba, Haiti, St. Vincent, Guyana and Jamaica. $6.95. (See Curricula for Teachers' Guide.) Friendship Press. (P,I)

Escape to the Jungle. Combination coloring book/story pages about radio outreach. FREE. Trans World Radio. (P,I)

From Arapesh to Zuni. Karen Lewis. Contains 26 short, easy-to-read stories of people groups, one for each letter of the alphabet. From William Carey Library and Wycliff. (See also Books)

George Mueller. #GS013. $8.50. A companion George Mueller Activity Lesson is also available (see Curriculum). Acorn Children's Publications. (I)

Global Prayer Digest, The. Published by the Frontier Fellowship at the U.S. Center for World Mission. A new story daily about a people group, or a missionary going to a people group. $1.00 for a single issue, or $9.00 subscription price per year, mailed to you (extra postage for Canada/Foreign). Available from The *Global Prayer Digest* Orders/Frontier Fellowship, U.S. Center for World Mission.

"Go Ye." #GS026. $8.50. A companion "Go Ye" Activity Lesson is also available (see Curriculum). Acorn Children's Publications. (I)

Gospel Ship Puppet Scripts. 105 page book of 24 excellent missionary scripts (see Activities/Puppets).

Happy Day for Ramona, A, and Other Missionary Stories for Children. Contains nine real-life, illustrated missionary stories from around the world. 51 pp. $3.99. Christian Publications (P,I).

Kiddy Leaflets. Each story/activity sheet is from a different country: Africa, Arabia, Brazil, China, Colombia, Egypt, France, Gambia, Greece, Guinea-Bissau, India, Indonesia, Italy, Ivory Coast, Japan, Mexico, Russia, South America, Spain, Sri Lanka, Thailand, Turkey, Venezuela, Zaire, Now & Then, and 5 Ways. Information on countries and cultures, with hands-on fun for children. Leaflets: 10 cents each plus 15 percent postage, or 7 for $1.00, or sample packet of 24 for $3.00, plus 15 percent postage; minimum postage charge: $1.00 per order. If order is over 200, price is 7 cents per leaflet. WEC International. (P,I)

Kid's World. See Activities—Crafts, Activities and Decorations.

Let's Look at... Series. Story/Coloring Books on **Korea, Malaysia, the Philippines, Thailand,** and **Indonesia**. 22 pages. See also Activities—Coloring. $1.95 each. OM F Books.

Making Missions Meaningful. Contains mission stories. From Pioneer Clubs. (See Books)

Mission Stories For Young Children. Barbara Oliver. 22 entertaining stories with simple yet concrete concepts. These stories for ages four through eight are perfect for children's sermons, church day care, Bible school, and more! 48 pages, $2.95. From New Hope.

Missions and Me. Karen Robertson and Bev Gundersen. Contains the complete set of 12 stories formerly in monthly kids' newspaper form, by Karen. An activity-filled way to learn about great historical missionaries and countries where they served. 50 pages. $6.95. From Monarch Publications. (I)

Money Idol, The. Adeline Char (Teachers' Swap Shop). A story about two Indonesian girls on the island of Java, whose family eventually turned from worshipping spirit idols, to the living God. Available FREE from Children's Missions Resource Center (P,I).

My Mom and Dad Are Missionaries. The story of the Mitchell Land family who serve in the Ivory Coast. $1.50. Teaching guide: $.75. Baptist Book Store Mail Order Center.

"No Longer My Son"–Malaysia. A 10-part story includes 10 reproducible pictures for coloring, map of Malaysia, memory verse and project ideas. About a boy in Malaysia who, after becoming a Christian, leads his father to Christ. $8.95. From Crossroads Publications. (P,I)

"Nothing But Trouble"–Guatemala. The 8-part story includes 8 reproducible pictures for coloring, map of Guatemala, memory verse and project ideas. Pedro goes to school with sore feet, encounters guerrillas and invites Jesus into his heart. $8.95. From Crossroads Publications, Inc. (P,I)

On the Big River. Pictorial story of a missionary family in Brazil. $1.20. Teaching guide: $.60. Baptist Book Store Mail Order Center.

Pink and Green Church, The, and Other Missionary Stories for Children. Contains nine real-life, illustrated missionary stories from around theworld. 51 pp. $3.99. Christian Publications (P,I).

Potato Story, The, and Other Missionary Stories for Children. Contains nine real-life, illustrated missionary stories from around the world. 53 pp. $3.99. Christian Publications (P,I)

Radio Kids! Quarterly story and activity newspaper. See Activities/Newspapers. Write for orders to Rosemarie Jaszka, Public Relations Dept., Trans World Radio. All ages.

Rat-Catcher's Son, The. Carolyn London. In their home in Nigeria, Sunday and her young brother, Little Lion, listen eagerly to their wise old grandfather, Baba, tell them stories. Each of the nine stories speaks to them about some situation which they face in daily life. See also Books. $4.20. SIM, USA. (P,I)

Reaching Brazil by Radio. Combination coloring book/story pages about radio outreach. FREE. Trans World Radio. (P,I)

Reaching the World By Missionary Radio. Combination coloring book/story pages about radio outreach. FREE. Trans World Radio. (P,I)

"Snakes, Witch Doctors and Prayer"–Liberia. The 8-part story includes 8 reproducible pictures for coloring, map of Liberia, memory verse and project ideas. Nyanpan faces snakes and a witch doctor in the Liberian Jungle. See how God answers the prayers of a mission school teacher. $8.95. From Crossroads Publications. (P,I)

"Strange Encounter, A"–India. The 8-part story includes 8 reproducible pictures for coloring. map of India, memory verse and project ideas. Children will love the adventures of Chako in India. $8.95. From Crossroads Publications. (P,I)

Sound of the Bell, The. $5.95. Janis Bell. (P)

Stories from Africa. SIM Authors, opt. cassette (also see Books). SIM.

Story of Ana, The. $1.95. Janis Bell. (I)

They Shall Be Mine. Fascinating stories of men and women who devoted themselves to spreading the word of God around the world. 135 pages. $7.50, from God's World Publications. (J,I)

World of Children's Stories, A. Anne Pellowski, editor. Children's stories, old and new from about thirty countries. They range from traditional folk tales and animal stories, to modern stories. $19.95. From Friendship Press.

Yono and Yanto's Christmas. By Adeline Char (Teacher's Swap Shop). A story of two Indonesian boys who illustrate forgiveness and accepting Jesus because of the Christmas story. Available FREE from Children's Missions Resource Center. (P,I,J)

4
ACTIVITIES

Coloring Books and Sheets

Back Home In Japan (activity). Student book to accompany **Back Home In Japan Teaching Guide.** $3.95. From OMF Books.

Color the Muslim World with Jesus' Love. Small, 18-page coloring/story book. FREE. From Center for Ministry to Muslims, or Kids Can Make A Difference. (P)

Coloring Book About the Andes. With stories. Family Book Center. (P,I)

Drawn to China. By Jim Ziervogel. A coloring/story book about China. $3.95. From OMF Books or Institute of Chinese Studies.

Escape to the Jungle. Flashcard/coloring pages. Trans World Radio. (P,I)

Jesus Loves the Children of the World. A book of reproducible multi-cultural patterns of children from 60 nations. Use these for bulletin boards, visualized songs and Bible verses, puppets, table decorations, flash cards, etc. Replaces the old 24- and 36-page versions. $7.95. Pattern Packs for the old versions are available at $2.75 each (12 pages). Bev Gundersen, Monarch Publishing. (P,I)

Let's Look at... Series. Books on **Malaysia,** the **Philippines,** and **Indonesia.** Each book is about 22 pp. and tells a story. $1.95 each. OMF Books.

MAF Helps People. Missionary Aviation Fellowship. Coloring/Activity book, telling a pictoral brief story about MAF's airplane ministry (12 pages). Cost unknown. Write to MAF.

Missionary Coloring Book, The. Contains John 3:16 written in 25 languages showing native costumes, flags, and map. Available from Bible Memory Association, and Kids Can Make A Difference. (P,I)

Reaching Brazil by Radio. Flashcard/coloring pages. Trans World Radio. (P,I)

Reaching the World by Missionary Radio. Coloring/storybook. Trans World Radio. (P,I)

What Language Does God Speak? Coloring book/story of Jo Shetler, Bible translator among the Balangao people of the Philippines. Wycliffe.

You Can Change The World Coloring Books: Two-Book Set. By Jill Johnstone. Two activity books each feature 11 countries and people groups from *You Can Change the World,* plus a world map showing the location of each country. Page references are given in brackets to help color in the pictures, find out more about the people involved—and start to pray for the world. Each 23 pages, and sold in sets only. STLAB/S, Discount $5.75. William Carey Library Publishers. (P,I)

Crafts, Activities, and Decorations

52 Fun Things Your Family Can do Together for Missions. Contains craft and activity ideas for the family. $1.25. Published by International Christian Fellowship. Available only from Children's Missions Resource Center.

52 Ways to Teach Children to Share the Gospel. By Barbara Hibshmann. Helps children learn to share the Gospel through puzzles, crafts, skits and special projects. From Rainbow Books. $9.95.

52 Ways to Teach Missions. Includes Come to the Missions Fair, mission dioramas, making missions banks, "Share A Spare" for Missions (a fun alternative for Halloween Trick or Treat), etc. Order from Rainbow Books. $9.95.

Activities and Crafts to accompany 15 stories from other publishers. $4.50 to $8.50 each. See also Curricula and Visual Aids. Send for price list to Acorn Children's Publications. (P,I)

Activity Books: Window to Alaska ($4.25), **Window to India, Window to Pakistan, Window to Kenya, Window to the C.I.S.** (formerly U.S.S.R.), **Window to Germany, Window to Mexico, Window to Japan, Window to Zaire,** and **Jesus Loves the Children of the World**. Bev Gundersen/Monarch Publishing. Reproducible activity pages for grades K-6 on food, holidays, religion, games, clothing, home life, and geography. Also contain puppet patterns and more, and are written so you can plug in facts from the mission(s) of your choice adapt them to your teaching goals. Request order form. From Monarch Publishing. (P,I)

Arabs: Activities for ElementarySchool Level, The. From Kids Can Make A Difference.

Can You Guess Brochure. A story-activity paper based on Bible translation. FREE. Indicate quantity desired. From Wycliffe. (P,I)

Carousel of Countries, A: Games, Songs, Recipes and Customs from Around the World. By Mary Kinney Branson. Contains recipes, games, customsm, songs, costumes, holidays, and other information about countries representing six continents of the world. New Hope Publishing. (P,I)

Chalkboard Catalog, The (1990-1991). Educational supplies catalog, listing supplies adaptable as missions education resources on 29 of its pages. Items include the following: Christmas Activities from Around the World, 4 sizes of world maps, several kinds of other cultures bulletin boards, flash cards from Places from Around the World, 3 sizes of inflatable globes, world map puzzles, World Map Outlines/duplicating master, and much more. For catalog write to: The Chalkboard.

Children Around the World Wall Hanging. 40" embroidered globe depicts children from 7 countries. $79.95. From Constructive Playthings.

Children's Language Brochure, The. Very interesting story-activity paper on Bible translation. FREE. Indicate quantity, available from Wycliffe Bible Translators. (P,I)

Children's World Series. Three books in this series include songs, games, and stories from around the world, which are fun to do. $52.50 for set of 3, but may be purchased separately. From Friendship Press. (Ages 5-12)

Christmas All Over the World. Handcrafted Advent Calendar, with embroidered international children, and Christmas symbols. Hanging is 16 1/2" wide x20" long. $39.95. From Constructive Playthings.

Count Your Way. Learn to count from one to ten in another language, phonetic pronunciation is provided. Item #135, $5.95 each. Indicate which ones you want: Africa (Swahili), Canada (French), Germany (German), Israel (Hebrew), Japan (Japanese), Mexico (Spanish), Arab world (Arabic), China (Chinese), India (Hindi), Italy (Italian), Korea (Korean), Russia (Cyrillic). Available from Kids Can Make A Difference.

Dining Customs Around the World. By Alice B. Mothershead, Garrett Park Press, Garrett Park, MD 20896. (I,J,A)

Dona Maria & Friends. From New Hope Publishing.

Drawn to China. (See Books.)

Embrace Your World. House to House, City to City, Nation to Nation. Missions Activities for families and home groups, written by Kathy Felty for Dove Christian Fellowship, Ephrata, PA. Activities designed for all ages, reproducible. Item #186, $5.00. Available from Kids Can Make A Difference.

Ethnic Celebrations Around the World. From Kids Can Make A Difference.

Faces of the Watching World. From Kids Can Make A Difference.

Fun Around the World. By Mary Branson. Games, crafts, food, and dress ideas you can use to help children experience the world. From Kids Can Make A Difference, and New Hope.

Globe Key Chains (metal) ($12/gross), **Plastic Earth Glide Balls** ($12/dozen), **Earth Squeeze Balls** ($9.60/dozen), **"Our Earth" slide puzzles** ($1.50/dozen). Catalog available. Available from Oriental Trading Company, P.O. Box 3407, Omaha, NE 68103-0407; 1-800-228-2269.

Great Global Activities. Bev Gundersen. A selection of hands-on activities that involve students as they study missionaries, nations, and people groups. Pattern pages are reproducible. 64 pages. $7.95. From Monarch Publishing.

Guess What I Made!?! Sharlande Sledge. Recipes from around the world offer a taste of missions. Illustrated, with aditional information about countries. Easy enough for older children to use on their own, younger children with help. $4.50. Baptist Book Store Mail Order Center. (P,I)

How to Make a "10/40 Window Display for Prayer." Contains a do-it-yourself instruction manual for an effective moving experience of "Touching the Nations." $3.00. From Esther Network International.

International Children Border. Vinyl border of 16 international friends with peel-away back, washable surface Two 33"x8" panels for a 66" long border. $19.95. From Constructive Playthings.

Junior Missionary Retreat. A 24-hour activity-filled missionary retreat for fifth and sixth graders. (See Curricula for description.) From One Way Street.

Kid's World. Quarterly story and activity leaflet. Teaching plans available with multiple-copy orders. First 25 FREE, after that, 10 cents each. CAM International. (P,I)

Kidscan Packet. Jan Bell. Includes the essential P-words with symbols on flashcards, sign, definitions, plus more. A Biblical worldview focused on God's Mission. Item #192, $9.95 includes postage. Kids Can Make A Difference. (P,I)

Listen To a Shadow. Zuverink and Haskin. Stories, photos, drawings and songs give small children a sample of the variety of languages Christian use to spread God's love in Indonesia. They use the language of batik, body language, music, the language of street sounds and other information. $2.95. From Friendship Press. (P)

Making Missions Meaningful. Has many craft suggestions. (See Books and Stories.) From Pioneer Clubs. (P,I,J)

Mission Action Book, The. Resource for mission action with suggested activities for adults, youth and children. $4.35. Baptist Book Store Mail Order Center. (All ages.)

Missions Alive. Role playing and crafts to accompany the ten-session series. (See Curricula.)

Missions Ideas. Includes songs, giving projects, stories, things to make and do, and much more to encourage children to be involved in worldwide missions. For all ages. Order item #0005, cost $12.00. Order from Sacred Literature Ministries. Also see Books.

Missions Made Fun For Kids: Creative Ideas to Involve Children in Missions. By Elizabeth Whitney Crisci. 128 pages of activities to help children to Think Missions now! It's not a "someday" calling. Creative ideas that will involve the children and young people in missions—global and local. Encourage, teach, and challenge missions awareness with fun activities that teach kids of all ages. DCC306-6, Discount $5.25. William Carey Library Publishers. (P,I,J)

My Missionary Friend's Diary. Nine-page booklet to assist children in praying for their missionary by keeping a record of various things about the missionary in the diary. Assists any children's group with long-term relationship with their missionary. Write to ask for sample diary and cost to: Crosswalk Resources or Kids Can Make A Difference.

"P-Words." Jan Bell. Integrate missions into your existing curriculum, by using these "P-Words." A unique and innovative teaching method, incorporating signs, symbols, and now music, to develop the concept of missions for kids. This method equips children with a Christian worldview that is focused on God's mission, enabling them to process what they're learning with critical thinking skills. See "Kidscan Packet." From Kids Can Make A Difference. (P,I)

Reach Around the World. Bob and Sandy Friesen. Contains 52 global awareness activities for youth, adaptable for 5th through 8th graders also. Includes cultural awareness games, missions food experiences, music, skits and more. Write for cost and information to Victor Books/SP Publications. (I,J)

Windows to the World and **More Windows to the World. Windows** includes units on China, Mexico, Australia, Brazil, British Columbia (Canada), West Germany, Egypt. **More Windows** deals with Norway, Japan, Kenya, Quebec, Italy, Peru, India. $10.95. From Good Apple, Inc., or Kids Can Make A Difference. (I)

Wordless Book. The salvation story without words, using 5 colored pages. Instruction leaflet, "How to Use the Wordless Book," included free with each book ordered. #4811097 2"x3", $.89; #4811101 3"x5", $1.50; #4811089 5-1/2"x7-1/2", $2.99 each. CEF Press.

World Children Calendar. Bev Gundersen. A multi-purpose book for 8-11-year-olds. Includes pictures and facts of children from 12 countries, puzzles, and Bible verses. Pages can be used as mini-posters. Reproducible filll-in calendar sheets can be used for any year and begun at any month. Stickers let kids keep track of special day. 34 pages. $5.95. From Monarch Publishing.

WorldTrek; 52 Missions Experiences for Children Grades 1-6. Lessons are a fun-filled journey through the fascinating world of missions, including hands-on experiences, stories, games, and activities. Lessons are age-graded and are flexible for 5 to 30 minutes. Only 8 or 9 lessons deal with cross-cultural experiences. From Worldfriends Press/WMU.

World Mission Activities. Nineteen learning activities that focus on who missionaries are and what they do. Janis Bell. (I)

Games

Best Board Games From Around the World. From Kids Can Make A Difference.

Friends Around the World game. Players race to get 16 International Friends to World Peace before the Blob. $20.95. From Constructive Playthings.

Games of the World. Familiar and new games from many different countries. Instructions tell how to make and play games for both adults and children. 282-page book, 9"x10-1/2". $16. From UNICEF. (All ages.)

Great Global Games. Bev Gundersen. Contains a variety of games to promote awareness of hidden people groups, missionaries and nations around the world. Activity pages are reproducible. 60 pages. $7.95. From Monarch Publishing.

Lost in the Rain Forest. A combination game/story—your mission: to find a lost Bible translation. The fun begins as the group makes decisions at each twist and turn in the story. Written by Ray Seldomridge, editor of Focus on the Family Clubhouse Magazine. Item #202, $6.95. Available from Kids Can Make A Difference.

Missions Games and Activities for Children. A collection of crafts, games and sports for children in grades 1 through 6. Baptist Book Store Mail Order Center. (P,I)

Prayer Spinner Game. A great way for children to pray over children's global concerns: poverty, false religions, war, laborers, praise, harvest, etc. $18.00. From Esther Network Int'l.

World of Children's Games, A. Mary Duckert. Over 100 games played by children all over the world. Number and age of players is noted for each, plus easy-to-follow rules. $19.95. From Friendship Press.

Games are also included with many stories and curricula.

Magazines, Newsletters, and Newspapers

Acorn'r. Missionary Newsletter for Children. Contains stories, photos, prayer suggestions and activities about missionary families, and missionary work. Write to Missionary Church. All ages.

CHAMP Program Missionary Mailing. The children's missionary club and bi-annual newspaper includes missionary stories, puzzles and games, articles about missions-related topics. Children may also write for additional materials such as crafts and missions lessons. **CHAMP** Program, Biblical Ministries Worldwide.

Children, Let Us Love! Every Fifth Child in the U.S. Faces Hunger. Five-page children's educational pamphlet to urge children to help the poor. Includes coloring pages, games, and Scripture, interspersed with facts about poverty and social programs for the poor. 75 cents each. From Reformed Church Press Distribution Center (see Publishers/Suppliers).

Children Vision International. Henry A. Villegas, M.D., FAAP, chief editor, and president of Children of Jesus Foundation, Inc. Magazine published quarterly by the International Society for Children and Youth Missions. Contains articles to provide physicians, dentists, health professionals, clergymen, educators, churches, organizations, other professionals and laymen with information on children's and youth outreach programs both home and abroad. See Resource Persons.

Evangelizing Today's Child, Official Publication of Child Evangelism Fellowship, Inc. Published bi-monthly. Features articles, stories, ideas for effective teaching, a complete lesson with visual-aid in each issue, and more—all for children's and missions teachers. From CEF Press.

Follow the Sun. Gweneth Deverall. Through the five story papers, children will share in the lives of the early Tahitian missionaries. Through stories, pictures and suggested activities, they will learn new words in new languages, and study about plants and animals on the islands. $3.95. From Friendship Press. (P, I)

God's World Books Educational Catalog (for Leaders and parents). Especially for Home Schoolers, contains a special missions books section from which to order many books at less than retail price. God's World Publications.

Kiddy Leaflets. Story/Activity paper sent regularly. See Stories for description. From WEC International.

Kids' World. Story paper for kids. From CAM International.

Radio Kids! Quarterly story and activity newspaper. Contains story, activity page, comic strip-style radio story, song, missions quiz, and letter to adults. Printed on brightly colored paper. No charge. Write for orders to Rosemarie Jaszka, Public Relations Dept., Trans World Radio. All ages.

White Fields for Young Workers. Paul and Marcy Griffo, publishers and directors. A newsletter for families and missions education leaders, dedicated to help them find their place of ministry in Christ's body, and in missionary work all over. See Resource Persons.

Projects, and Fund Raising

10 Practical Ways For Kids to Have Significant Involvement in the Muslim World. From children's "pen pal" ministry to sending a package of treats to an MK, there are ideas for one or a whole class to do. Send for this and more ideas to Frontiers Associates.

All God's Children. (See Curricula.)

Bank. World Bank. Four-inch diameter on 1-inch base. $.75. Baptist Book Store Mail Order Center.

Banks for Projects. Available FREE from Conservative Baptist Foreign Mission Society. (All ages)

Dime Cards. Slotted folders hold money for mission projects.

World Bank. For special offerings.

PACT Bank. Raise money for Plant-A-Church-Together program for overseas church buildings.

Mr. Page Bank. A book-bank for overseas literature projects.

Rice-Bowl Bank. For Good Samaritan Program.

Be a Missionary at Home! Mail Gospel Letters to the homes of Muslims in Turkey! Letters are mailed by volunteers or children's groups (a missions project)! Friends of Turkey provides addresses and materials. Your group supplies envelopes, postage, pray over them, and mail them. Write to Friends of Turkey.

Be a Pen-Pal and Share the Gospel! Share the Gospel with Turkish Muslims! Friends of Turkey recruits students (children or young people) who want to correspond in English. 99 percent of people in Turkey are followers of Islam. An exciting opportunity for children's groups to make friends and witness to an Unreached People Group! For both of the above write and ask for brochures: Friends of Turkey.

Children Caring for Children. (See Curricula.) Children raise funds to send Bibles and New Testaments to other countries. The Bible League.

Providing Bible Lessons and Bibles for those who respond to radio broadcasts. Gospel Missionary Union. May use with their two flashcard stories. (P,I).

VBS Missions Projects. Write to HCJB.

Skits, Dramas

SKITuations, Vol. XII: The Missionary. Steve and Cora Alley. 139-page double-book, due to extra copies of skits. Slapstick adventures of four characters. Contains coloring pages, discussion questions, crafts, crossword puzzles and more. $20.00. From SKITuations. (I,J,A)

5
VISUAL AIDS

Flags.

3'x 5' cloth flags of various countries come in sets of eight. Allow eight weeks for delivery. Order from Area CBFMS Offices. Call CBFMS Headquarters to find number of your local area office. $8.00 per set rental plus shipping.

U.S. Flags, State Flags, Custom Banners, Foreign Flags: in sizes from 3'x5' to 8'x12'. Also small spearhead flags. As for 32 page color catalog. From U.S. Flag Supply, Inc.

Flannelgraph

• **Children of the World**. Fifteen large children in colorful costumes. $10.00. Kids Can Make A Difference. (P).

Christian Soldier, The. Brian learns how the armor of the long-ago soldier is like the armor God has provided for him against his enemy, Satan, in this single lesson, which can be used in a 30-minute setting, or 90-minute extended time. $4.49. From CEF Press. (P,I)

Families on Felt.

Black family—$5.50 (#LF818)

Hispanic family—$5.95 (#LF823)

Oriental family—$5.95

Caucasian family—$5.95

Available from KALEIDOSCOPE.

Forever Friends—Pretty Pals. Dress these like paperdolls, except they are flannel. Lindsey (Caucasian), #5501, $5.95; Mikko (Oriental), #5502, $5.95; Keisha (African-American), #5503, #5.95; Maria (Hispanic), #5504, $5.95. From KALEIDOSCOPE.

Horizons Never End. A single flannel lesson about "Ro" Rochunda Pudaite, who was born as a pagan in India, and grew up to become the president of an international missionary organization. $4.49. CEF Press. (P,I)

How the Dyaks Learned to Give. One or two lessons teaching how the Dyaks in West Borneo learned the concept of giving sacrificially. C E F Press. $4.49. (P,I)

"I Dare." Five-part story of Amy Carmichael's dedicated, courageous life as a missionary in India. Portrayed in a simple, but attention-holding presentation. $9.99. C E F Press. (P,I)

Men God Used. Contains three lesson stories from the lives of Jonathan Goforth, George

Mueller, and Hudson Taylor. $8.50 (#MMGK). Available from: BCM International. (J,I)

"So Send I You." History of missions in seven lessons. Includes missionary stories of Jesus, Paul, St. Patrick, Crusaders, Raymond Lull, Count Zinzendorf, Brainerd, and Judson in 46 colorful flannel figures and 16'x25' world map. $6.50. BCM Int. (I)

World Map (Flannel). (See also Maps)

Flashcards

Abessende. God saves and provides for an African girl. Needs to be colored and mounted on cardboard if necessary. $3.50(includes S&H). Baptist Mid-Missions Women's Department.

Adventure in Brazil. A true story centered around the adventure-loving son of American missionaries to Brazil, told in ten chapters, 44 illustrations. #5010. $9.95 plus $2.75 shipping. Bible Visuals, Int'l. (P,I)

Andrew and the Hurricane. Five-part story from Jamaica. Needs to be colored and mounted on cardboard if necessary. $3.50(includes S&H). Baptist Mid-Missions Women's Department.

Annie, Iowa Farm Girl. True testimony. Needs to be colored and mounted on cardboard. $3.50 (includes S&H). Baptist Mid-Missions Women's Department.

Antonio of Brazil/The Walking Umbrella. Two true one-chapter stories. A black boy in Delaware uses an umbrella to explain salvation. Antonio, a boy in Brazil, tells the Gospel to friends by using the story of "The Walking Umbrella." 20 illustrations. #5585. $6.95 plus $2.75 shipping. From Bible Visuals International. (P,I)

Big Storm, The. Brotherly love in Chad, Africa. Needs to be colored and mounted on cardboard. $3.50 (includes S&H). Baptist Mid-Missions Women's Department.

Brother Andrew, God's Smuggler. Five lessons in 10"x13" flashcard book, true story of sharing the Word of God behind the Iron Curtain is adapted from the book *God's Smuggler* by Brother Andrew. Order item #MBA, $4.75 plus $3.50 shipping from BCM Publications Int. (P, I)

Charles Studd. A five-lesson full-color flipchart on the life of CT Studd, great for VBS. $12.00. From WEC International Media Dept. (I,J)

Chosen Friend, A: A Story of Mexico. Indian culture, opposition to and reception of the gospel are seen through the eyes of Rosa, an Aztec Indian, in this 5-chapter story based on true accounts. 25 illustrations. Item #5090. $8.95 plus $2.75 shipping. Bible Visuals, Int'l. (P,I)

Clean Wash, A. Illustrates the caste system in India. Needs to be colored and mounted on cardboard. $3.50 (includes S&H). Baptist Mid-Missions Women's Department.

Devil-Kings and Cannibals. A thrilling 5-chapter story from the life of John Paton, pioneer missionary to New Hebrides Islands. 40-page flashcard. $9.99. CEF Press. (P,I)

Doctor in the Pygmy Forest. Five-chapter story of Dr. Carl Becker, missionary physician in Zaire for 47 years. Tells of God's power, guidance, and deliverance, as he encounters witch-doctors, leprosy, pygmies, and war. 32 illustrations. Item #5095, $8.95, plus $2.75 shipping. Bible Visuals Int'l. (P, I.)

Doming the Popsicle Boy. A story of the Philippines. Ten-part story of how Doming, from a Muslim background, finds Christ as his Savior and then helps to win his grandfather. 40 illustrations. Item #5100, $9.95 plus $2.75 shipping. Bible Visuals, Int'l. (P,I)

Door that Opened, The. A Chinese boy comes to know the Lord. Needs to be colored and mounted on cardboard. $3.50 (includes S&H). Baptist Mid-Missions Women's Department.

Faun and the Naughtiest Pig/Boy from Mindoro. One story about Thailand, and one from the Philippines. $8.95. OMF BOOKS. (P,I)

Freedom from Fear. Superstition among the Navajos in Arizona. Needs to be colored and mounted on cardboard. $3.50 (includes S&H). Baptist Mid-Missions Women's Department.

From Darkness to Light. A Navajo boy finds release from fear. Needs to be colored and mounted on cardboard. $3.50 (includes S&H). Baptist Mid-Missions Women's Department.

Gaston, The Love Servant. True story from Chad, Africa. Needs to be colored and mounted on cardboard. $3.50 (includes S&H). Baptist Mid-Missions Women's Department.

Go Ye. Illustrated story to accompany the lessons "Go Ye," both available from Acorn Children's Publications. $8.50. (P,I)

God's Bridge. Story of Africa. A one-chapter story showing the various ways people try to prepare themselves for heaven: money, education, and more. Twelve illustrated pages. Item #5140, $5.95 plus $2.75 shipping. From Bible Visuals Int'l. (P,I)

HCJB, Shortwave Goes a Long Way. Tells the story of Billy and his friend who discover the world and Jesus Christ via shortwave radio. Terrific way to teach children how the power of the gospel transcends cultural barriers. $6.00. World Radio Missionary Fellowship, Inc. (see HCJB).

His Best For God. A single lesson about Eric Liddell, the great Olympic champion, and his commitment to God for full-time Christian service in China. $4.49. CEF Press. (P,I)

How Turea Kept Christmas/Penny and the Christmas Star. The story of a girl in Morocco who turned her back on Mohammed to serve the living and true God—and how she "kept Christmas." 14 colored illustrations. **Penny** learns from the Wise Men that the King desires the love of her heart, her prayers, and her obedience. 10 colored illustrations. Available also in Spanish. Size 10"x14". #5425. $7.95 plus $2.75 shipping. Bible Visuals Int'l. (P,I)

Hudson Taylor. The venture of faith that led a young lad to China and later enabled him to influence a hundred other missionaries to follow. Includes missions verse and song suggestions. 10"x13" spiral bound. Five lessons in 40-flashcard pages. $9.99. From CEF Press. (P,I)

John and Betty Stam. K. Weitzel. Five-part story of the famous missionary martyred in China. 33 ilustrations. $8.95 plus $2.75 shipping. From CEF Press, Bible Visuals Int'l., and OMF BOOKS. (P,I)

Ladi and White-White. Two stories from Africa: **Ladi** hears the gospel and courageously witnesses to her father; **White-White**, a lost lamb, rehearses the love of the Good Shepherd for His sheep. 20 illustrations. Item #5250, $5.95 plus $2.75 shipping. Bible Visuals, Int'l. (P,I)

Laraba and Audu. Two stories of Africa. **Laraba** is a warm, true illustration of God dealing with His children; **Audu** reveals the trials involved before and after conversion. 24 illustrations. Item #5270, $6.95 plus $2.75 shipping. Bible Visuals, Int'l. (P,I)

Living Word in Italy, The. A bandit hears God's Word. Needs to be colored and mounted on cardboard. $3.50 (includes S&H). Baptist Mid-Missions Women's Department.

Ly Huy's Escape. Story of Viet Nam. Five-part story telling how Ly Huy and his sister escape the soldiers, then are introduced to the Savior by a missionary and reunited with their mother. Includes song and 5 chapters; 24 illustrations. Item #5275, $6.95 plus $2.75 shipping. Bible Visuals, Int'l. (P,I)

Madjou. How Madjou found the Savior in Africa through a missionary nurse. Needs to be colored and mounted on cardboard. $3.50 (includes S&H). Baptist Mid-Missions Women's Department.

Madugu. One-part story about a Nigerian boy who hobbled into a mission station, finding a cure for his sore leg as well as for his sinful heart. $5.79. C E F Press. (P,I)

Man for God's Plan, A. A single lesson from the life of Jim Elliot whose commitment to Christ led hhim to martyrdom in Ecuador. $4.49. CEF Press. (P,I)

Martiniana. Five-part story of a Warao Indian girl from Venezuela. Needs to be colored and mounted on cardboard. $3.50 (includes S&H). Baptist Mid-Missions Women's Department.

Miracle for Samuelito, A. A Story of Mexico. Samuelito receives Christ as his Savior and experiences another miracle—the answer to a long-sought desire. Six chapters, 40 illustrations. Item #5280, $8.95 plus $2.75 shipping. Bible Visuals, Int'l. (P,I)

Missionary Stories About.... Flashcard series of "real-life" stories from around the world. Includes 8 sets of 13 stories, 52 flashcards per set. Stories alone are $5.95 per set. See Curriculum for students' and leader's guide. From Randall House Publications. (P,I)

Mustapha's Secret. A five-part story about a boy in a Muslim culture in Morocco, and the opposition he faces from his family when becoming a Christian. Helps children (and adults) unravel some of the "mysteries" of Islam. $10.95. (see also Curricula) Available from CEF Press and GMU. (P,I)

Nathan Finds New Life in Jerusalem. Nathan moves to Jerusalem and meets Ali, an Arab Christian boy, in this 10-chapter story teaching salvation, Jewish customs and more. 40 illustrations. Item #5320, $9.95 plus $2.75 shipping. Bible Visuals, Int'l. (P,I)

New Life for Iromo, A. Five-part story about an African girl in Sudan who suffers much through the cruelty of her parents and the witch doctor. $6.50. BCM Int.

No Darkness at All. Hamid and his blind sister live in North Africa. He turns to the "Light of the World" and returns to his village to witness. Five chapters, 40 illustrations. Item #5340, $9.95. Bible Visuals, Int'l. (P,I)

On Wings of Song. A plane brings the Gospel to a remote village in Brazil. Needs to be colored and mounted on cardboard. $3.50 (includes S&H). Baptist Mid-Missions Women's Department.

Praying Hyde. Illustrated biography of John Hyde, a missionary to India. Known for his earnest prayer life, will movtivate students to pray. Five chapters, 20 illustrations. Item #5480, $5.95 plus $2.75 shipping. Bible Visuals Int'l. (P,I)

Rejoicing With Joy. A single lesson on the exciting story of Joy Ridderhof, founder of Gospel Recordings. Includes take-home puzzle and games. $4.49. CEF Press. (P,I)

Ringu of India's Forest. Children will quickly make friends with Ringu in this exciting story set in the Kurku villages of central India. 40 flashcard pages. $9.99. From CEF Press.

Roberto. About a lad from the jungles of Brazil. Needs to be colored and mounted on cardboard. $3.50 (includes S&H). Baptist Mid-Missions Women's Department.

Run, Ma, Run! The spellbinding story of Mary Slessor, a woman born in the slums of Scotland who became a great missionary leader in Africa. Five chapters in 40 flashcard pages. $9.99. From CEF Press. (P,I)

Salvation and Sea Worms. Story of Fiji. Five-part story in which the message of salvation is woven around the Fijian customs of firewalking, the sea worm festival and others. 20 illustrations. $6.95 plus $2.75 shipping. Bible Visuals, Int'l. (P,I)

Seiko and the Spider's Thread. Five-part illustrated story with setting in Japan. $8.95. OMF BOOKS. (P,I)

Send Someone To Tell Me! A single powerful lesson about Oliofa, a young boy from New Guinea who receives specific answers to prayer. He learns to pray for his needs and for the missionaries in this 30- to 90-minute lesson (extends it to extended hour lesson). $4.49. From CEF Press. (P,I)

Surrounded By Headhunters. A five-chapter true story based on the ministry of Frank and Marie Drown to the Shuar (Jivaro) Indians in Ecuador. Oversized (11"x17") flashcard book. Text also in Spanish. $10.95. (See also Curricula) From CEF Press and GMU. (P,I)

Tamenta. A true five-part missionary story from the jungles of Surinam, South America. $4.50. BCM Int.

Three Stories from India. $9.50. BCM Int.

Ti-Fam: Witch Doctor's Daughter, chooses Christ over superstition in this fascinating five-chapter story based on the land of Haiti. 40 flashcard pages. $9.99. CEF Press. (P,I)

We Two Alone. Ten-part story of Ruth Hege and Irene Ferrel in Congo. $3.00 (includes $1.00 postage and handling). Baptist Mid-Missions Women's Department. (I)

Yandicu: From Witch Doctor to Evangelist. Jeanette Windle & Jan Clements of Gospel Missionary Union. In five lessons, follow Yandicu Salinas, the Guarani Indian in Boliva, South America, who was changed from witch doctor to evangelist after hearing the gospel from a GMU missionary. Text also available in Spanish. $10.95. (See also Curricula). From CEF Press, and GMU. (P,I)

Yangsan Starts a Church. The conversion and prayers of a Korean grandmother. Needs to be colored and mounted on cardboard. $3.50 (includes S&H). Baptist Mid-Missions Women's Department.

Young Ki's Courage/Sold Twice. Stories of Korea and Malaysia. $8.95. OMF BOOKS. (P,I)

Globes

Earth Globe. Inflatable, heavy-duty vinyl globe, 36" diameter. $11.95. Constructive Playthings.

Earth Squeeze Balls ($9.60/dozen). From Oriental Trading Company.

Globe Key Rings. Miniature globe on keyring @ $.20 each or $1.80/dozen. Available from KALEIDOSCOPE .

Globes, rigid, cloth, stuffed and inflatable, all sizes, colors and types (see maps). From Pasadena Map Co.

Globes, rigid, cloth, stuffed and inflatable, all sizes, colors and types (see maps). From The Chalkboard.

Earth Globe. Inflatable, heavy-duty vinyl globe, 36" diameter. $11.95. From Constructive Playthings.

"Globall," soft and huggable stuffed cloth globe with the "10/40 Window" drawn on it. Children, big and little toss and say: "Catch the vision! Get global!" A great prayer tool to give children of the world a hug from Jesus, as they pray over the countries and people groups of the world. $25.00. From Esther Network, International.

Globe, full-color inflatable, with stand, 18" diameter vinyl. Teach children to pray for people groups and missionaries. $11.99, ask for #S6615. Available from Walter Drake, 127 Drake Building, Colorado Springs, CO 80940. Or call 1-800-525-9291.

Hug-A-Planet, soft, huggable globe. It is 14" in diameter, colorfully screen-printed on durable fabric, softly stuffed, for $14.95. Available from KALEIDOSCOPE, (For globe key chains, see Activities, Decorations)

Hugg-A-Planet, Earth, is a cuddly, soft, stuffed globe. Colorful, non-toxic inks, printed on 100% coltton cloth, detail oceans and continents. This one is small (6"), $13.00 (92638Z), from UNICEF.

Metal Globe Key Chains, ($12/gross). Available from Oriental Trading Company.

"Our Earth" slide puzzles, ($1.50/dozen). From Oriental Trading Company.

Plastic Earth Glide Balls, ($12/dozen). Oriental Trading Company.

Variety stores and educational supply stores also carry globes.

Maps

Atlas of the World. Hardcover, 160 pages. Considered the best atlas for all-around family use. Includes many photos, and population figures and maps right on the pages of the maps. From God's World Publications.

"Bibles for All" world map (40"x28"). Has pictures of Unreached People Groups around the border, plus much other information on the linguistic situation of the world. Request #WCL001, $2.00. From William Carey Library Publishers.

Language Project Maps (Indicate which): Liberia, Sierra Leone, Cameroon. Maps list and locate current projects and give population estimates. From Lutheran Bible Translators. (I,A)

Map, large. Angel's School Supply.

Map, World Missions. $7.99. From Gospel Light.

Map of China. Includes information about China's people groups. ($6.00) Institute of Chinese Studies.

Maps, all sizes, world, country, umbrella maps, jacket maps, atlases and much more. From Pasadena Map Co. Call for prices.

Maps, all sizes, world, country, puzzle maps, Mini Hugg-a-Planet, map outlines and much more. Send for catalog from The Chalkboard.

Maps, all sizes. Warren's Educational Supplies.

✒ **Pray for the World.** A beautifully presented and completely updated map of the world. Full color Hammond map. Discount price, $2.50. From OM LIT.

World Atlas for Young People. 100-page hardcover book (8 1/2"x11"), for ages 9-14, $13.00 (#88953B). Available from UNICEF (see Activities/Games or Publishers/Sources).

World Map. Flannel map is large (27"x36"), handy to use on flannel board, and with flannel-graph stories. Costs $5.50 (#FB26). Available from BCM Publications.

World, Outline Map. $.75. Baptist Book Store Mail Order Center.

World. (52"x34"). RM008. God's World Publications.

World Map placemats. Brightly colored custom laminated, measuring 17 1/2"x12", all countries, capitals, major cities, oceans, etc. Two for $5.98 plus $2 postage & handling, or save on 4 for $9.99 plus $2 postage & handling. From Geography Placemats.

World Placemat. Excellent laminated, placement size, colorful countries on one side, and blank white countries on other side, for coloring or filling in details or names. 1993 copyright map has up-to-date clearly printed names and bright colored countries. $3.00 each plus shipping. From Christopher Reber.

Posters and Pictures

Children and Water Photos on the UNICEF's 1995 calendar. The theme is the use of water in natural settings in many different countries all over the world. 57 full-color photographs with ample space for calendar notes. Four-language edition. $13.50, from UNICEF.

Children of the World Pack. 18 posters of children of other lands. On the back of each poster, questions and cultural information spark discussion, writing projects and more. Size 11"x16". $29.95 for pack. Lakeshore Learning Materials.

Foreign Missions Preschool Pictures. Twelve teaching pictures for teachers. Order #6331-62. $4.25. Baptist Book Store Mail Order Center. (P)

Missions Pictures for Preschoolers. Two sets, each with twelve beautiful 11"x14" color photographs of missions at home and abroad. Set 1 order #6330-20; Set 2 order #6333-85; $7.25 each. Baptist Book Store Mail Order Center. (P)

People of the World. Peter Spier. Giant wall poster (3'x8'). A treasure chest of knowledge for discussions and activities. Available laminated. Adaptable for all ages. From Anatomical Chart Company.

Peoples Profiles Prayer Cards. Colorful greeting-card style photo-info cards, featuring an Unreached People Group, for prayer. Inside is a brief profile of the people group, a simple map, and facts about the group. Seven cards available so far, sold singly or in 10-card packs of one design: **Bihari, Fulani, Kashmari, Thai, Turkman, Uighurs, Uzbeks.** Useful for correspondence, missions display or for children to pray for. $1.85 each, with discounts for quantity orders. Avaible in packs and envelopes also available. Adaptable for all ages. Available from William Carey Library Publishers.

Unreached Peoples 1990 Poster. Facts and figures from around the world in bright, colorful poster form. $3.00 for 2; $1.00 each additional; add $2.00 processing fee per order. William Carey Library.

Versatile Visuals For Salvation. Contains 26 pictures: Christ, crosses, open tombs, Heaven and many others in full color. For cutting out to illustrate stories and lessons. $3.19. CEF Press.

Children, World Full of. Standard Publishing.

World's Children. Book contains 25 children's figures in national dress, 8 large international heads for paper bag puppets and 25 smaller heads, all for cut-outs. $3.19. CEF Press.

Puppets

Brochure/Price List: Puppets, Patterns, Scripts, other free materials. Puppet Pals.

Catalog: Puppet Ministry. Bible-True Audio Visuals.

Catalog, Puppets (black, white, Asian, Hispanic, and Native American) and Information. Catalog, $2.00. One Way Street.

Catalog: Puppets and Supplies. Puppet Productions.

Catalog: Puppets and Supplies for Ventriloquist\Puppet Ministry. Includes instructions, dummies, scripts, puppets, patterns, tapes, resource books, newsletter. FREE. Maher.

Catalog: Puppets, Patterns and Scripts. Includes animal puppets as low as $14.99. FREE. The Arklings.

Easy-to-Make Puppets. Fran Rottman. 192-page resource book contains over 100 puppet patterns, simple illustrated directions, and dozens of ways to use puppets as creative teaching tools. Some of the types of puppet directions include those made of clothespins, wooden spoons, paper plates, paper bags, boxes, gloves, rods, fingers, socks, hand puppets, marionettes, and more. Ask for PMR-23, $16.95. From One-Way Street.

Easy-to-Make Puppets and How to Use Them. (EC) $7.99. From Gospel Light.

Finger Puppets. Individual puppets: African, Eskimo, Mexican, Muslim, Polynesian—Puppet + story, $3.00. **Unreached People Group puppets:** Tribal, Hindu, Chinese, Muslim, Buddhist—available **only** in set of 5 puppets + story, $12.00. Include P & H, $3.00. From MLB DESIGNS. Ages 3-10.

Hand Puppets. Five different ones. $14.95 each or 5 for $69.95. Gospel Light/Harvest Publishing. (P,I)

Paper Bag Puppets. Two sets available. Gospel Light Publishers. (P,I)

Stick Puppets. 9"x12" faces. Each set includes 5 stick puppets, song sheet with several songs, and description for each puppet. (#LF401) for Mexican, black boy, American Indian, Japanese, & Dutch—set is $12.95. (#LF402) for Hawaiian, black girl, Eskimo, Israeli, Anglo white boy—set is $12.95. Available from KALEIDOSCOPE.

Books/Booklets/Printed Materials/Misc.

Gospel Ship Puppet Scripts. #GN005, 105 pp., contains 24 excellent missionary scripts. ACORN Children's Publications. (P,I)

Houses for Mouse Finger Puppets. Grace Harp, $1.00. Puppet Pals.

How to Use Mouse Finger Puppets. Grace Harp, $1.50. Puppet Pals.

Puppet Scripts on Missions. Eight puppet scripts with missions themes. Scripts use from 2 to 4 characters, and are 2 to 6 minutes in length. (PS-06) $8.00. From One Way Street.

Using Puppets Effectively. Grace Harp, $1.95. Puppet Pals.

6
AUDIO-VISUALS

Cassettes

Adventures of Luju, The (Africa). Ethel Barrett. (Record) (P,I)

I Am A House Of Prayer. (see Music, Audiocassettes)

Jesus Loves Me, Too. (see Music, Audiocassettes)

Kids Talk. Focuses on missionary radio (dramas, music, children's letters). For ages 6-12. From Trans World Radio.

Kuta Story, The. A 5-part true story of a Muslim boy who became a Christian when he and his sister secretly listened to radio broadcasts. Indonesia. $6.00. Kids Can Make A Difference.

Mission Friends Cassette Tape. Four songs about missions sung by children. For 4's and 5's. $7.95. Baptist Book Store Mail Order Center. (P)

Missionary Adventure Stories, Tape 1. Ethel Barrett. $7.99. Gospel Light. (P,I)

Missionary Adventure Stories, Tape 2. Ethel Barrett. $7.99. Gospel Light. (P,I)

Snake Stories from Africa. Book and cassette: $5.70. SIM, USA. (P,I)

Stories from Africa. Book and cassette: $6.15. SIM, USA. (P,I)

For Leaders:

Fantastic Missions Festivals. Nadine Starner. A highlight address from an ACMC national conference. For general and youth leaders. Item # SC 693. $4.95 for members/$6.95 for non-members. From ACMC/Publishers.

Impacting Kids For Missions. Barbie Campbell. A highlight address from an ACMC national conference. For children's leaders. Item #SC694. $4.95 for members/$6.95 for non-members. From ACMC/Publishers.

Missions Education for Kids. Geri Templeton. A highlight address from an ACMC national conference. Filled with practical ideas to use in missions education. For children's leaders. Item #SC432. $5.00; non-members, $6.95. From ACMC.

Film Strips

Many Faces of Korea, The. An American child visits Korea and learns about the churches and Baptist work in Korea. 51 frames. Baptist Book Store Mail Order Center. (P,I)

Missionary Projects for Vacation Bible School. Used for past VBS projects. Also request information on current VBS projects. Conservative Baptist Foreign Mission Society. (P,I)

Nigeria, Home for Brian. Brian, a young boy, shows what life is like as an MK (missionary kid) living in Nigeria. 56 frames. Baptist Book Store Mail Order Center. (P,I)

Films

Humpty. 25-minutes. Color. Rent: $42.00. International Communications. (P,I,J) (Also available in video.)

Last Out, The. 28 minutes. Color. Rent: $42.00. International Communications. (P,I,J)

Little Lost Fisherman. 28 minutes. Color. Rent: $39.00. International Communications. (P,I,J)

Mysterious Book. 28 minutes. Color. Rent: $30.00. International Communications. (P,I,J)

Tanglewood Secret. 80 minutes. Color. Rent: $84.00. International Communications. (P,I,J)

Treasure in the Snow. 90 minutes. Color. Rent: $129.00. International Communications. (P,I,J)

Slides

Amy and Nicole. 13 minutes. Story of a French girl. Includes script and cassette. Rent: $10.00. Purchase: $29.95. Also on video. Home Ministries Department, WEC International Media Dept. (P,I,J)

Carlos of Colombia. 10 minutes. Includes script and cassette. Rent: $10.00. Purchase: $29.95. Also on video. Home Ministries Department, WEC International Media Dept. (P,I,J)

Gaga of Zaire. 15 minutes. Includes script and cassette. Rent: $10.00. Purchase: $29.95. Also on video. Home Ministries Department, WEC International Media Dept. (P,I,J)

Kids Can Be Missionaries Too. This 5-minute slide/tape program explains what it means to be a missionary and the importance of children sharing their faith. Rent: Free-will offering. Purchase: $20.00. Also in video. CAM International, Home Ministries Dept. Also from CBFMS (order from area offices). (P,I)

Mussa of North Africa. 12 minutes. Includes script and cassette. Rent: $10.00. Purchase: $29.95. Also on video. Home Ministries Department, WEC International Media Dept. (P,I,J)

Som Chai of Thailand. 11 minutes. Includes script and cassette. Also on video. Rent: $10.00. Purchase: $29.95. Home Ministries Department, WEC International Media Dept. (P,I,J)

That Others May Hear. 10 minutes. Introduces children to the concept of people groups and the need for missionaries. Includes script and cassette. Also on video. Rent: $10.00. Purchase: $29.95. Home Ministries Department, WEC International Media Dept. (P,I,J)

What Does God Want With A Kid Anyway? Slide Story of Chet Bitterman, martyred missionary in Columbia, SA, in 1981. Short and geared to a child's level. Write and ask for cost. From BCM International, c/o Media Ministries. (P,I)

What Language Does God Speak? Seven minutes. K. Lewis and P. White. Companion coloring book available. The story of Bible translation among the Balango People Group in the Philippines, based on the story of Jo Shetler. Excellent! Rent: $5.00. Wycliffe Bible Translators. Also on Video. (P,I)

Videos

Amy and Nicole. (see Slides) 13 minutes. Rent–$10.00 or purchase–$17.95 from WEC Int'l.

And It Was Good Soup! An award-winning presentation about faith in God's Word among the Yessan-Mayo people of Papua New Guinea. 33 minutes. Free on a loan basis, but donation appreciated. From Lutheran Bible Translators. (J-A)

Bantu. The thrilling story of an African boy who runs away from home. A missionary helps his wounded foot and tells him the Gospel story. 15 minutes. $15.75. CEF Press. (P,I)

Carlos of Colombia. (see Slides) 10 minutes. KIDSCAN has prepared a lesson guide to enhance discussion. Carlos' family is faced with difficult choices now that they are Christian. Item #182, $15.00. From Kids Can Make A Difference, or $17.95 from WEC Int'l.

Children Caring For Children. One 10-minute video for each country studied: Romania, China, Brazil, Russia/Ukraine, and Philippines (See Curricula, to use with videos). The Bible League. (P,I)

Children's Missionary Stories. Contains 3 former slides stories: **Before the Moon Dies** (13 min.), **Ian and the Gigantic Leafy Obstacle** (13 min.), and **How Mr. "I Don't Feel Like It" Lost His Name** (9.5 min.). Order #4414. $8.95. All ages. OMF Books.

Days of Discovery. Part of the VBS kit by the same name. Includes five 5-minute video programs designed to fit easily into the daily schedule. See Curricula. Good New Productions.

First Valentine, The. (12 Minutes) Story of a man determined to make a difference in a pagan culture that prohibited Christian marriages. $19.95. Kids Can Make A Difference. (P,I)

"Flights For Kids" video. Accompanies "Flights For Kids" curriculum (optional), but also available separately. Contains 3 five-minute segments which take children on a voyage to some of the world's most remote areas and introducing them to the unique ministry of MAF. Available for $6 donation from MAF.

Gaga of Zaire. (see Slides) 15 minutes. Rent–$10.00, or purchase–$17.95. From WEC Int'l.

God's Kaleidoscope. Color. 12 minutes. Communicates the need for God's Word in every language. Purchase: $10.50 (discount) from William Carey Library, and $15.00 from Wycliffe (ask for rental fee). Song sheet, "God's Kaleidosope," comes with video.

Hidden Island. 15-minute video or film, in English or Spanish, is about 2 boys in Panama. An excellent, dramatic film. Write for information and prices to Lakeland Child Evangelism Ministries, Inc., PO Box 612, Winona Lake IN 46590. (219)594-5344.

Humpty. (See Films for description.) Glenray Communications.

Impacting Kids For Missions. Barbie Campbell. (For leaders.) ACMC 1992 children's missions seminar, explaining how to develop your own missions education curriculum. VHS format, 63 min. (VC 780) ACMC member discount price $24.00. Regular price $34.00. Write or call ACMC.

Kambari. 22 minutes. With Nigerian youth, Gracie, the viewer's world is expanded to include the Kambari peoples, an unreached Nigerian group. Great music. Order item #184. $29.95 plus 15% S&H. Kids Can Make A Difference. (J,I)

Kids Can Be Missionaries Too. The same as the slide/tape (See Slides). For rent for a free-will offering, or purchase for $8.00. From CAM International.

Lion Territory. In the inner city Daniel finds himself fighting till he lets the Lord take control. His gang notices the difference when he receives Christ. 7 minutes. $15.75. CEF Press. (P,I)

Malay Kids. 10 minutes. From slides of Malaysia. Focuses on a Muslim girl, Shirifa. $12.00. Kids Can Make A Difference.

Mussa of North Africa. (see Slides) 12 minutes. Rent–$10.00, or purchase–$17.95. From WEC Int'l.

Operation Coconut. 21 minutes. A missionary kid in the Philippines. $29.95. Kids Can Make A Difference. (J,I)

Patna Kids. From Kids Can Make A Difference.

Peace Child. Taken from the popular book *Peace Child* by Don Richardson. Features how Don and his wife explained the gospel to a Stone-Age headhunting people who held treachery as their highest virtue. 30 minutes. DRB001, $20.50 (disc.), from William Carey Library. Good for all ages.

Pedro and the Bright City. Adventure story of a Peruvian boy who narrowly escapes death in a fall over a cliff, then learns about Jesus from a missionary. 13 minutes. $15.75. CEF Press. (P,I)

Rescue In Manila. High-drama cross-cultural film features Kevin, son of missionary parents, Rina, an orphaned girl, and Julio, member of a street gang. 18 minutes. From Lakeland CEM Office.

Rick-a-Chee Series. All six books on video, two stories per video (See Books). When purchasing the videos, the ready-to-color books are an optional purchase. Video #1: (2 story books) **Rick-a-chee and the Runaway Kobos** and **Rick-a-chee anda Puppy**; Video #2: **Rick-a-chee and the Monkey Stick** and **Big Trouble for Rick-a-chee**; Video #3: **Rick-a-chee Takes A Journey** and **Rick-a-chee and the Sky-Blue Hat.** Prices: 1 video–$15, 1 video + 2 books–$20, 2 videos + 4 books–$40, 3 videos + 6 books–$59, 3 videos only–$42. From SIM USA.

Sugarcane Island. About Haitian sugarcane workers, focusing on the various roles missionaries have in today's world. $29.95. Available from Kids Can Make A Difference.

Six Stories from WEC. (all on one video). **Amy and Nicole**(13 min.), **Carlos of Colombia**(10 min.), **Mussa of North Africa** (12 min.), **Gaga of Zaire** (15 min.), **Som Chai of Thailand** (11 min.), **That Others May Hear** (10 min.). Rent: $15.00; purchase: $29.95. WEC International Media Dept. (P,I)

Som Chai of Thailand (above). 11 minutes. KIDSCAN has prepared a teacher's lesson guide to expand it into a longer teaching session. Som Chai, a Buddhist boy, finds opposition from family and friends when he gives his heart to Christ. Illustrated. Item #7, $15.00. From Kids Can Make A Difference, or $17.95 from WEC International Media Dept.

That Others May Hear. (see Slides) 10 minutes. Rent–$10.00, or purchase–$17.95. WEC Int'l.

With Their Own Eyes. NEW! After centuries of oppression and domination, the Quiche people of Ecuador find new hope and freedom through the Gospel as it is revealed to them through the written Word of God for the first time. 13 minutes. $15 purchase or free loan, but donation appreciated. From Lutheran Bible Translators. (J-A)

Word Has Arrived, The. Tells the story of Bible translators at work in Papua New Guinea. Filmed on location. An edited version of **"And It Was Good Soup!"** 16 minutes. Free on a loan basis, but donation appreciated. From Lutheran Bible Translators. (J-A)

FOR LEADERS:

Impacting Kids For Missions. Barbie Campbell. A VHS video cassette tape of past ACMC national conference for children's leaders. Item #VC 780. Members: $24.95/non-members: $33.95. From ACMC (see Publishers).

KIDSCAN Video. Jan Bell. This workshop on video enables you to train teachers and parents. Presents Jan demonstrating the P-words to children and adults with easy-to-use teaching methods. Item #139, $49.95. Price includes a "Kidscan Packet." From Kids Can Make A Difference (For Leaders).

7

SONGS, MUSIC

Musicals and Audiocassettes

Charlie Cherub. Go Into All the World. It's missions conference time and Charlie Cherub takes the kids on a trip to Eastern Europe. Tape–$8.99, songbook–$4.95. Kids Can Make A Difference.

Heart To Change the World. A missions musical for children in the second grade and up. Cassette tape and songbook are published by Maranatha! Music. Ask for prices, from Word, Inc.

I Am a House of Prayer. Includes "House of Prayer March," "House of Prayer Rap," "Window of the World," and "Catch the Vision," with the second side just instrumental. $7.00. **House of Prayer** sheet music also with all the same songs. $5.00. From Esther Network International, and Kids Can Make A Difference,

Jesus Loves Me, Too. Audiocassette for grades 1-6 to go with Baptist India Curricula for 1992. Includes Indian music and Indian language versions of familiar children's songs. 15 minutes. #4447-52. $4.95. Order or purchase from a nearby Baptist Book Store Center.

Kid's Praise! 6. In this musical, Psalty the Songbook stresses the importance of meeting the spiritual and physical needs of people around the world. Songbook contains lyrics, music, dialogue, and choreography. Songbook (KCM-63SB) $4.50, cassette (KCM-63) $9.95, cassette soundtrack (KCM-63AS) $55.00. Excellent! From One Way Street (P,I).

M-I-S-S-I-O-N-A-R-Y That's Us! Linda Peterson. A children's cantata that involves the entire church. Includes six songs. Book: $3.25; performance cassette: $5.95; accompaniment cassette: $18.95. Christian Publications.

Mission Friends Cassette Tape, for fours and fives. Four songs about missions sung by children. $7.95. Baptist Book Store Center.

This is Missions, and Seven Other Missions Songs. Richard Farmer. Original missions songs for children on cassette tape; songbook is also available from RAF Ministries Inc.

World of Praise, A, with Mr. Globe and Jeffrey. Children's songs sung from 10 different different countries. From Mission Vision Network/FEBC.

Songs

Amamas Long Jisas Ol Taim (Papua-New Guinean Pidgin English; to tune of "Rejoice in the Lord." Pronounce phonetically.)

Deus Amamas long Jisas oftaim,　Nau gen Mi amamas

Amamas long Jisas oltaim,　Nau gen mi amamas

Amamas, amamas,　Anu gen mi amamas

Amamas, amamas,　Na gen mi amamas.

B-I-B-L-E, The*

The B-I-B-L-E　It has one story you see,

La Biblia　To reach all nations with God's love,　The B-I-B-L-E.

Cristo Me Ama (Spanish; "Yes, Jesus Love Me")

Cris-to me a-ma (3x),

La Biblia dice a-si.

(Pronunciation guide: Cree-sto may-aa-ma, La Bee-blia dee-say aa-see.)

Deus e' Tao Bom (Portuguese; "God is So Good")

Deus e' tao bom (3x), e' tao bom pra mim.

　(God is so good (3x), He's so good to me.)

Cristo e' re-al (3x), e' re-al pra mim.

(Christ is real , He is real to me.)

El-e vol-tara' (3x), voltara' pra mim.

　(He will return , He'll return for me.)

Dispela De (Papua-New Guinean Pidgin English; to tune of "This is the Day")

Dispela de, dispela de,　God I bin wokim, God I bin wokim

Yumi amamas,　Yumi amamas

God I stap wantaim mi,　God I stap wantaim mi

Dispela de, dispela de,　God Ibin wokim.

Far Away (Reprinted by permission of Betty Paul.) Write for music and suggestions for illustrating song from Children's Missions Resource Center.

1) Far away, Far away　Lives a child I do not know

God knows him, God loves him,　loves his child I do not know.

2) Jesus died, Jesus died　For this child I do not know

God says "Go", God says "Go"　to this child I do not know.

3) I must go, I must tell   This dear child I do not know

I must give, I must go,   tell of Him who lovs us so.

Far, Far Into Europe

(Tune: "Wide, Wide As the Ocean")

Far, far into Europe,   In heathen lands in the East.

Deep, deep, into Africa   The Gospel is preached.

Although I'm not wealthy,

Still in God's work I may share.

By what I give to Him,

Others may hear of Him - everywhere.

"God's Kaleidoscope," Debbie Rettino, is the lovely song sung by children on the video by the same name. Write and ask for the sheet music from Wycliff.

Hari Ini (Indonesian; "This is the Day")

Hari ini,   Hari ini

Hari nya Tuhan,   Hari ya Tuhan.

Mari kita,   Mari kita

Bursuka Ria,   Bursuka Ria.

Hari ini,   hari nya Tuhan.

Mari kita, Bursuka Ria.

Hari ini,   Hari ini

Hari nya Tuhan.

(Pronunciation: ha-ree eenie, Too-haan, maa-ree kee-ta, Ber-su-ka Ree-a.)

If You're Blessed To Be A Blessing*

(Tune: "If You're Happy and You Know It, Say Amen!")

1) If you're blessed to be a blessing, clap your hands (2x)

If you're blessed to be a blessing,

then your life will surely show it.

If you're blessed to be a blessing, clap your hands.

2) ...stomp your feet

3) ...say AMEN!

4) ...do all three.

Jesus Loves Them*

Jesus loves the na-tions	Every tongue and every tribe
H-e wants to u-se you	To reach them to be His Bride.

Yes, Jesus loves them, (3x)

The Bible tells me so.

Jesus Loves The Unreached Children*

Jesus loves the unreached children,

All the unreached children of the world.

Muslims, Buddhists, Hindus, Chinese, Tribals need Him too.

Jesus died for all the children of the world.

*(by permission of "Destination 2000")

Jesus Wants New Friends (to tune of "The Farmer In the Dell")*

Jesus wants new friends, Yes, Jesus wants new friends,

I will bring a friend to Him, Yes, Jesus wants new friends.

Game Actions: Walk in circle, holding hands. On third line teacher chooses child to stand in center.

A friend will bring a friend, A friend will bring a friend,

A friend will bring a friend to Him, Yes, Jesus wants new friends.

Game Actions: Walk in circle. On third line center child chooses another friend to join him. Repeat v. 2 until all children are chosen.

And now we're all His friends, And now we're all His friends,

And that's the way the world should be, Yes, now we're all His friends.

Game Actions: All stand in center while singing.

*(by permission of Judy Theriault)

John 3:16 (good at Christmas)

(to tune of "Silent Night.")

John 3:16. John 3:16.

(For) God so loved the world that He -

Gave His on-ly be-got-ten Son, (that)

Who-so-e-ver be-lie-veth in Him

Should not per-ish but ha-ve-

E-ver-las-ting life.

Lai Shin Yesu (Chinese; "Come to Jesus")

Lai shin Yesu (3x), Shan zai.

(Come to Jesus (3x), Right now.)

Shan zai lai shin Yesu,

(Right now come to Jesus;)

Lai shin Yesu shan zai

(Come to Jesus right now.)

Mi Laikim Yu Jisas (Papua-New Guinean Pidgin English; to tune of "Oh, How I Love Jesus")

Mi laikim yu,   Mi laikim yu Jisas

Yu bikpela bilong mi.

(pronounce phonetically.)

Nzambi Ke Mbote (Kituba language, Zaire; "God Is So Good")

Nzambi ke mbote, (3x)   Ke mbote na mono!

Pikinini, Pikinini (Pidgin Chorus from Papua New Guinea, sung to the tune of "Follow, Follow, I Would Follow Jesus" (pronounce phonetically.)

Pikinini, pikinini,   Yu laik kam long Jisas.   Susa, brata, Papa wantaim mama.

Liklik pila,   bik pela,   Jisas laikim yu.   Ol i kim long Jisas, Em i laikim yu.

Waga Shu Iesu (Japanese; "Yes, Jesus Loves Me")

Wa-ga Shu I-e-su, (3x)

Wa-re o aa-i-su.

(Pronunciation guide: Wah-gah shoe Ee-yes-su, Wah-ray oo aa-ee—sue.)

Yumi Kristen (Papua-New Guinean Pidgin English; to tune of "I Will Make You Fishers of Men.")

Yumi Kristen ritim Baibel

Tingting long em, mekim beten.

Ritim Baibel, mikim beten long olgeta de.

Bilong kamap strong bilong daunim sin.

Ritim Baibel, mekim beten long olgeta de.

(Pronounce phonetically.)

Source Books/Visualized.

Easy-to-Learn Missionary Songs. John and Lorella Rouster. Contains Kituba (Zaire) words to familiar tunes of three choruses/songs. Also 5 English-language missionary-oriented songs set to familiar tunes. FREE. Every Child Ministries.

Growing Songs For Children. Only missionary songs listed here. C E F Press.

> Stop-Go-Watch—#42.
>
> Good News—#46 (substitute "ALL" for "I" and "me")
>
> Go Ye Into All the World—#50.
>
> From Pennsylvania to California—#51.
>
> Remember All the People—#52.
>
> We Have a Story to Tell—#53.
>
> Lord, Send Me!—#54.
>
> Turn from Your Idols—#55.
>
> Here am I, Send Me—#56.
>
> How Shall They Believe?—#57.

House of Prayer sheet music containing House of Prayer March, House of Prayer rap, Window of the World, and Catch the Vision. See Audio-cassette. $5.00. From Esther Network, International.

It's a Big, Big World. Large colorful visualized and illustrated song helps children realize that in this big world, there're many people who don't know Jesus. $6.29. CEF Press.

Missionary Chorus Books, one each for children and for adults, about 30 songs in each. From Lakeland Bible Mission, Inc.

Salvation Song Books #1. Only Missionary songs listed. C E F Press.

> The Children's Friend—#2.
>
> Be A Missionary—#9.
>
> Jesus Loves the Little Children—#19.
>
> Bring Them In—#64.

Salvation Song Books #2. Only Missionary songs listed. C E F Press.

> God's Way—#9.
>
> "Go Ye Into All The World"—#21.
>
> Little Missionaries—#22. (Substitute tune of "Jesus Loves Me.")
>
> The Children of a Thousand Tongues—#24. (Change words to "Two Thousand Tongues.")
>
> I Will Go—#26.

Salvation Song Books #3. Only Missionary songs listed. C E F Press.

> To The Whole World Go!—#2.
>
> Go and Give and Pray—#54.
>
> To the East, To the West—#55.
>
> Jesus Loves Children—#56. (For "Hidden Peoples" theme song, change last three words in song from "far away lands" to "hidden peoples.")
>
> A Missionary Prayer—#57.
>
> Missionary Echo—#58.
>
> Jesus Loves the Little Children—#59.

Salvation Song Books #4. Only Missionary songs listed. C E F Press.

> All The Children Ought To Know—#2.
>
> Go Seek Them, Go Find Them, Go Win Them—#3.
>
> Let Compassion for Children—#4.
>
> Capture the Children for Christ—#5.
>
> Go Bring in the Children—#7.
>
> Offering Response—#13.
>
> A Little Missionary—#48.
>
> It Isn't Fair—#55.
>
> Missionary Chorus ("Young Folks, Old Folks")—#79.

Sing, Children, Sing. Carl S. Miller, editor. 72 pp. Contains songs, dances, and singing games of many lands and peoples. $3.50, by arrangements with UNICEF. Quadrangle/The New York Times Book Co.

Songs Around the World, from **Fun Around the World** (see Activities). Two pages contain easy songs to familiar tunes.

This is Missions, and Seven Other Missions Songs. Richard Farmer. Original missions songs by the composer that are especially geared to children. Cassette tape is also available from RAF Ministries Inc.

World of Children's Songs, A. Mary Lu Walker, editor. Over 100 fun songs from countries around the world. Most have at least one stanza in the original language. Appropriate for home, church, and classroom. $19.95. From Friendship Press.

Note: Most new songs are better taught when illustrated on tagboard, or with overheads. Use motions and choreography as appropriate.

Additional missionary and cross-cultural songs are in many of the curricula.

8

Index of Places

(Materials Dealing with Places or with People from those Places)

Afghanistan

    Visual Aids—Flashcards. **Visualized Missionary Stories**.

Africa

    Curricula.

        Children Caring for Children.
        World Christian Curriculum.

    Books.

        Adventures In Africa.
        Adventures of Tonko.
        It Was Always Africa.
        Snake Stories from Africa.
        Stories from Africa.
        What Will Tomorrow Bring?

    Stories.

        Stories From Africa.

    Visual Aids—Flashcards.

        Abessende.
        Big Storm, The.
        Gaston, The Love Servant.
        God's Bridge.
        Ladi and White-White.
        Laraba and Audu.
        Madjou.
        No Darkness at All (North Africa).
        Run, Ma, Run! (Mary Slessor)
        Visualized Missionary Stories.

    Audio-Visuals—Videos.

        Bantu.
        Children Caring For Children.
        Rick-a-Chee Series (3 videos in Series).

    Audio-Visuals—Slides and Videos. **Mussa of North Africa.**

    Audio-Visuals—Cassettes.

        Adventures of Luju, The.

Missionary Stories.
Snake Stories from Africa.
Stories from Africa.

Alaska

Curricula. **World Christian Curriculum.**

Books. **Harley Shields, The.**

Activities—Crafts, Activities and Decorations. **Activity Books: Window to Alaska.**

Andes

Books. **Catch a Wild Pony, Climb a Mountain Peak.**

Activities—Coloring Books. **Coloring Book About the Andes.**

Arab World

Activities—Crafts, Activities and Decorations. **Count Your Way Through...the Arab World.**

Argentina

Visual Aids—Flannelgraph. **Santo, Boy of Argentina.**

Asia

Curricula. **Neighbors Near and Far: Asians in Asia and North America.**

Books. **Ten Missionary Talks on Southeast Asia.**

Australia

Books.
Children of the World: Australia.
Family in...Australia.
Sandy: the Girl Who was Rescued.

Activities—Crafts, Activities and Decorations. **Windows to the World.**

Bangladesh

Books. **Chayna, the Girl No One Wanted.**

Bolivia

Curricula.
Adventures in Peru and Bolivia.
It Happened in Bolivia.
Yandicu: From Witch Doctor To Evangelist (also Flashcards).

Books.
Children of the World—Bolivia.
Down a Winding Road.

Brazil

Curricula.
Adventure In Brazil (to accompany Flashcard).
Children Caring for Children (Brazil).

Books.
By An Unfamiliar Path.

> **Carlos: the Street Boy Who Found a Home.**
> **On the Big River.**

Stories.
> **Reaching Brazil by Radio.**

Activities—Crafts, Activities and Decorations. **Windows to the World.**

Activities—Coloring Books. **Reaching Brazil by Radio.**

Visual Aids—Flashcards.
> **Adventure In Brazil.**
> **Antonio of Brazil/The Walking Unbrella.**
> **Carlos of Brazil.**
> **On Wings of Song.**
> **Roberto.**

Songs, Music—Songs. **Deus e' Tao Bom.**

British Columbia (Canada)

Activities—Crafts, Activities and Decorations. **Windows to the World.**

Burma

Books.
> **Ann H. Judson.**
> **Golden Foot.**
> **Ropes to Burma.**

Burundi (Africa)

Books. **What Will Tomorrow Bring?**

Calabar (Nigeria)

Curricula, and Flashcards. **Run, Ma, Run.**

Cambodia

Books. **Edge of Conflict.**

Chad (Africa)

Books. **Unaware of an Angel.**

Visual Aids—Flashcards.
> **Big Storm, The.**
> **Gaston, The Love Servant.**

China

Curricula.
> **Children Caring for Children (China).**
> **Escape By Night.**

Books.
> **Drawn to China (also an Activity book).**
> **East Into Yesterday; Jeff Andersen Series #1.**
> **East of the Mistry Mountains; Jeff Andersen Series #2.**
> **East of the Shifting Sands; Jeff Andersen Series #3.**
> **From Here to There and Back Again.**
> **J. Hudson Taylor: For God and China.**

   Li Hua: The Girl Who Found Acceptance.
   On the Clouds to China.
  Activities—Crafts, Activities and Decorations.
   Count Your Way Through...China.
   Windows to the World.
  Visual Aids—Flashcards.
   Door that Opened, The.
   Hudson Taylor.
   John and Betty Stam.
   Visualized Missionary Stories.
  Visual Aids—Maps. China.
  Audio-Visuals—Videos. **How Mr. "I Don't Feel Like It" Lost His Name** (one part of a 3-story vidio).
  Songs, Music. **Lai Shin Yesu**.

Colombia
  Books.
   By An Unfamiliar Path.
   Columbian Jungle Escape.
   Doña Maria and Friends.
   Donald Orrs, The: Missionary Duet.
  Audio-Visuals—Slides and Videos. **Carlos of Colombia**.

Congo
  Books.
   Boy of the Congo Forest.
   House Beyond Congo Cross, The.
   Mbambi that Had No Ears, The, and Other Congo Stories.
  Visual Aids—Flannelgraph. **Doctor in the Congo**.
  Visual Aids—Flashcards. **We Two Alone**.

Cuba
  Books. **The Caudills: Courageous Missionaries.**

Denmark
  Books. **Nikolai: the Boy Who Ran Away**.

Ecuador
  Curricula. **Surrounded By Headhunters** (also Flashcards).
  Books.
   Culture Guide: Ecuador.
   Heart for Imbabura, A.
  Audio-Visuals—Videos. **With Their Own Eyes**.

Egypt
  Books. **Family in...Egypt**.
  Activities—Crafts, Activities and Decorations. **Windows to the World**.

El Salvador

Books. **Visiting in the Global Village, Volume 1 (El Salvador, Tanzania, Japan).**

Fiji

Visual Aids—Flannelgraph. **Raju, Fire Walker of Fiji.**

Visual Aids—Flashcards. **Salvation and Sea Worms, Story of Fiji.**

Finland

Books. **Children of the World–Finland.**

France

Audio-Visuals—Slides and Videos. **Amy and Nicole.**

Germany

Curricula. **World Christian Curriculum.**

Activities. **Windows to the World.**

Greece

Books. **Children of the World–Greece.**

Guatemala

Stories. **"Nothing But Trouble"–Guatemala.**

Haiti

Visual Aids—Flashcards. **Ti-Fam: Witch Doctor's Daughter (Haiti).**

Audio-Visuals—Videos. **Sugarcane Island.**

Honduras

Books. **Dr. Harms, the Helper.**

Houston, Texas (USA)

Books. **Always a Friend.**

India

Curricula.

Friends of India.
"I Dare." (Amy Carmichael)
Let's Go To India.
My Friends in India.
Praying Hyde.
Ringu of India's Forest. (also Flashcards)
Welcome To India.

Books.

Amy Carmichael.
Amy Carmichael: Let the Little Children Come.
Children of the World–India.
Doctor Who Never Gave Up, The.
Family in...India.
God's Madcap (Amy Carmichael).
Happiness Under the Indian Trees.
Whistling Bombs and Bumpy Trains.

Stories.
> "Strange Encounter, A"–India.

Activities—Crafts, Activities and Decorations. **More Windows to the World**.

Visual Aids–Flannelgraph.
> **Horizons Never End (Rochunga Pudaite)**.
> **"I Dare" (Amy Carmichael)**.

Visual Aids—Flashcards.
> **Clean Wash, A**.
> **Praying Hyde**.
> **Ringu of India's Forest**.
> **Three Stories from India**.
> **Visualized Missionary Stories**.

Audio-Visuals—Film Strips. **Children Caring For Children**.

Indonesia

Curricula.
> **Indonesia: Islands of Flowers, Elephants, and Change/ Children's Packet**.
> **World Focus; Muslim People Groups–Indonesia**.

Books.
> **Broto**.
> **Children of the World–Indonesia**.

Activities—Coloring Books. **Let's Look at...Indonesia**.

Activities. **Listen To a Shadow**.

Songs, Music. **Hari Ini—Song**.

Iran

Books. **Tales of Persia**

Israel

Curricula.
> **Nathan of Israel** (also Flashcards).
> **World Christian Curriculum**.

Italy

Activities—Crafts, Activities and Decorations. **More Windows to the World**.

Visual Aids—Flashcards.
> **Living Word in Italy, The**.

Ivory Coast

Books. **My Mom and Dad Are Missionaries**.

Visual Aids—Flashcards. **Namango of the Ivory Coast**.

Jamaica

Visual Aids—Flashcards. **Andrew and the Hurricane**.

Japan

Curricula.
> **Aki and the Banner of Names (and optional Teachers' Guide)**.

An American Child Visits Japan.
Back Home in Japan.
Trip To the Land of the Rising Sun, A.
World Christian Curriculum.

Books.
Ai-Chan's Secret.
Bobby In Japan.
John andJulie Go to Japan.
Kazuko's Family.
Family in...Japan.
Visiting in the Global Village, Volume 1 (El Salvador, Tanzania, Japan).

Activities—Crafts, Activities and Decorations.
Activity Books: Window to Japan.
Count Your Way Through...Japan.
More Windows to the World.

Visual Aids—Flashcards. **Seiko and the Spider's Thread.**

Songs, Music. **Waga Shu Iesu—Song.**

Jordan

Books. **Children of the World–Jordan.**

Kenya

Books. **Chebet and the Lost Goat.**

Activities—Crafts, Activities and Decorations. **More Windows to the World.**

Korea (South)

Curricula.
Mi Jun's Difficult Decision.
Won Gil's Secret Diary.

Books. **Children of the World–South Korea.**

Activities—Coloring Books. **Let's Look at...Korea.**

Visual Aids—Flashcards.
Yangsan Starts a Church.
Young Ki's Courage/Sold Twice (first part is of Korea).

Audio-Visuals—Filmstrips.
Many Faces of Korea, The.

Latin America

Curricula.
Neighbors Near and Far: Hispanic North America and Latin America.
Through Latin America.

Songs, Music—Songs.
Cristo Me Ama.
Deus e' Tao Bom.

Liberia

Stories. **"Snakes, Witch Doctors and Prayer"–Liberia.**

Macao
>   Curricula. **Escape By Night.**
>   Books. **Matthew's Dad is a Missionary.**

Malaysia
>   Books. **Children of the World–Malaysia.**
>   Stories. **"No Longer My Son"–Malaysia.**
>   Activities—Coloring Books. **Let's Look at...Malaysia.**
>   Visual Aids—Flashcards. **Young Ki's Courage/Sold Twice** (second part on Malaysia).

Mexico
>   Curricula. **Samuelito** (also Flashcards).
>   Books.

>> **Children of the World–Mexico.**
>> **Down a Winding Road.**

>   Activities—Crafts, Activities and Decorations.
>> **Activity Books: Window to Mexico.**
>> **Windows to the World.**

>   Visual Aids—Flashcards.

>> **A Chosen Friend.**
>> **A Miracle for Samuelito.**

>   Songs, Music. **Cristo Me Ama**—Song.

Micronesia
>   Books. **Danger in the Blue Lagoon/Din Be Still.**

Morocco
>   Curricula and Flashcards.

>> **Mustapha's Secret.**
>> **No Darkness At All.**

>   Books. **Family In ...Morocco.**
>   Visual Aids—Flashcards. **How Turea Kept Christmas/Penny and the Christmas Star.**

Mozambique
>   **Adventures in Africa.**

New Hebrides Islands
>   Curricula and Flashcards. **Devil-Kings and Cannibals.**

New Zealand
>   Books. **Children of the World–New Zealand.**

Nigeria
>   Stories. **The Rat-Catcher's Son.**
>   Books.
>> **Adventure in Nigeria.**
>> **Hattie Gardner: Determined Adventurer.**

Yakubu.
Visual Aids—Flashcards. **Madugu (Nigeria)**.
Audio-Visuals--Filmstrips. **Nigeria, Home for Brian**.

North America (Indians)
Curricula.
Crickets and Corn.
Our Friend, Kee Yazzie.

North America (Mexican-Americans)
Curricula.
I Am Important.
Our Amigos in America.

Norway
Activities. Crafts, Activities and Decorations. **More Windows to the World**.

Oman
Books. **Family in...Oman**.

Pakistan
Books. **Family in...Pakistan**.
Visual Aids—Flashcards. **Secret Search, The**.

Papua-New Guinea
Visual Aids—Flashcards. **Send Someone To Tell Me!**
Audio-Visuals —Videos.
And It Was Good Soup.
The Word Has Arrived.
Songs, Music—Source Books. **Five Pidgin English Choruses from Papua-New Guinea**.
Songs, Music—Songs. **Yumi Kristen**.

Paraguay
Books. **Two Dreams and a Promise**.

Peru
Curricula. **Adventures in Peru and Bolivia**.
Books.
Down a Winding Road.
Family in...Peru.
Activities. Crafts, Activities and Decorations. **More Windows to the World**.
Audio-Visuals —Videos. **Pedro and the Bright City**.

Philippines
Curricula.
Children Caring for Children (Philippines).
Pearl Makers (and optional Teachers' Guide).
World Christian Curriculum.

Books.

    Children of the World–Philippines.
    Whistling Bombs and Bumpy Trains.

Activities—Coloring Books.

    Let's Look at...the Philippines.
    What Language Does God Speak?

Visual Aids—Flashcards.

    Doming the Popsicle Boy.
    Faun and the Naughtiest Pig/Boy from Mindoro (second story from Philippines).

Audio-Visuals—Slides. **What Language Does God Speak?**

Portugal

Visual Aids—Flannelgraph. **Antonio, Fisherman of Portugal.**

Songs, Music—Songs. **Deus e' Tao Bom.**

Romania

Curricula.

    Children Caring for Children (Romania).
    Trapped In Darkness.

Russia/Ukraine

Curricula.

    Children Caring for Children (Russia/Ukraine).
    Courage For a Cross (and Teachers' Guide).

Activities. Crafts, Activities and Decorations. **Count Your Way Through...Russia.**

South Africa

Books.

    Rosa, Child of Destiny.
    Escape From the Darkness.
    Mystery of the Scar.

Spain

Books. **Children of the World–Spain.**

Sudan

Curricula. **A New Life For Iroma.**

Books. **Family In...Sudan.**

Surinam, South America

Visual Aids—Flashcards. **Tamenta.**

Sweden

Books. **Children of the World–Sweden.**

Switzerland

Books. **Antoine and the Magic Coin.**

Tahiti

Activities—Story Papers. **Follow the Sun.**

Taiwan

Curricula. **Taiwan's Urban Working Peoples.**

Books.

From Here to There and Back Again.
Happiness Under the Indian Trees.
Oz and Mary Quick: Taiwan Teammates.

Tanzania

Books. **Visiting in the Global Village, Volume 1 (El Salvador, Tanzania, Japan).**

Thailand

Books.

Before the Moon Dies (also on Video).
Children of the World–Thailand.
The Gods Must Be Angry.

Activities—Coloring Books. **Let's Look at...Thailand.**

Visual Aids—Flashcards.

Faun and the Naughtiest Pig/Boy from Mindoro (first story from Thailand).
Visualized Missionary Stories.

Audio-Visuals—Slides and Videos. **Som Chai of Thailand.**

Audio-Visuals—Videos. **Before the Moon Dies** and **Ian and the Gigantic Leafy Obstacle,** (two parts of a 3-story Video).

Tibet

Books. **Dawa Bema: the Uncertain Monk.**

Turkey

Venezuela

Visual Aids—Flashcards. **Martiniana.**

Vietnam

Books. **Din Be Still/Danger In the Blue Lagoon.**

Visual Aids—Flashcards. **Ly Huy's Escape from Viet Nam.**

Zaire

Visual Aids—Flashcards. **Doctor in the Pygmy Forest.**

Audio-Visuals—Slides and Videos. **Gaga of Zaire.**

Songs, Music—Songs. **Nzambi Ke Mbote.**

Songs, Music—Source Books. **Easy-to-Learn Missionary Songs.**

Zimbabwe

Audio-Visuals—Videos. **School Someday.**

Index of Peoples
(Materials Dealing with Specific People Groups)

Balangao People

    Activities—Coloring Books. **What Language Does God Speak?**

    Audio-Visuals—Slides and Videos. **What Language Does God Speak?**

Bibleless Peoples (26)

    Books. **From Arapesh to Zuni.**

Buddhist Peoples–Japanese

    Curricula.

        A Trip to the Land of the Rising Sun.
        An American Child Visits Japan.
        World Focus; Buddhist People Groups–Japan.

Chinese Peoples

    Curricula.

        Escape By Night.
        World Focus; Chinese People Groups–China.

Dyak Peoples of West Borneo

    Visual-Aids--Flannel. **How the Dyaks Learned to Give.**

Guarani Indians of Bolivia

    Curricula and Flashcards. **Yandicu.**

Hindu Peoples

    Curricula.

        "I Dare."
        World Focus; Hindu People Groups–India.

    Books.

        Child of Destiny.
        Escape From the Darkness.
        Mystery of the Scar.

Hispanic Peoples of North America

    Curricula.

        I Am Important.
        Neighbors Near and Far: Hispanic North America and Latin America.
        Our Amigos in America.

Indian Peoples of North America

    Curricula.

        Crickets and Corn.
        Our Friend, Kee Yazzie.

Jivaro People (Ecuador)

    Curricula and Flashcards.

        Surrounded By Headhunters.

Kituba People

Songs, Music—Songs. **Nzambi Ke Mbote**.

Songs, Music—Source Books. **Easy-to-Learn Missionary Songs**.

Kuta People

Audio, Cassette—**The Kuta Story**.

Muslim Peoples

Curricula.

Indonesia: Islands of Flowers, Elephants, and Change Children's Packet.
Journey to Uzbekistan (Uzbeks).
Mustapha's Secret (also Flashcards) (Muslims in Morocco).
Secret Search, The (Pakistan).
World Focus; Muslim People Groups–Indonesia.

Books. **Tales of Persia.**

Visual Aids—Flashcards. **How Turea Kept Christmas/Penny and the Christmas Star.**

Activities—Coloring Books. **Color the Muslim World with Jesus' Love.**

Audio-Visual—Cassettes. **The Kuta Story (Indonesia).**

Audio-Visual—Slides and Videos. **Mussa of North Africa.**

Navajo People

Curricula. **Our Friend Kee Yazzie.**

Books. **Mud on Their Wheels.**

Visual Aids—Flashcards.

Freedom from Fear.
From Darkness to Light.

Quiche People

Audio-Visuals—Videos. **With Their Own Eyes.**

Tribal Peoples

Curricula. **World Focus; Tribal People Groups (Mexico).**

Warao People

Visual Aids—Flashcards. **Martiniana.**

26 Bibleless People Groups

Books.

From Arapesh to Zuni.
You Can Change the World.

Various People Groups

Audio-Visual—Slides and Videos. **That Others May Hear.**

Audio-Visuals—Videos. **God's Kaleidoscope.**

9

Index of Children's Mission

Resource Publishers/Suppliers

Accent Publications, P.O. Box 36640, 7125 Disc Drive, Colorado Springs, CO 80936. Phone 719-535-2905; to order: 800-525-5550; FAX: 719-535-2928.

Curricula. **Tot Time: Missionaries Tell About Jesus**.

Books—For Leaders. **Missions Made Fun For Kids.**

ACMC (Advancing Churches In Missions Commitment) P.O. Box ACMC, Wheaton, IL 60189-8000. ACMC sales order line: 1-800-798-ACMC(2262), FAX: 708-260-0285. In Canada: Box 474, Sta. W, Toronto, Ontario, M6M 5C1 CANADA.

Curricula.
Is This Missions Thing For Real? (youth)
Mini Missions Conference For Children. (series of booklets)
Who Is a Missionary? (complete kit)
Who Is a Missionary? (book only)

Books—For Leaders.
I Don't Want to Wait Until I'm Grown Up.

Audio-Visuals—Cassettes.
Fantastic Missions Festivals.
Impacting Kids For Missions.
Missions Education for Kids.
Audio-Visuals—Video.
Impacting Kids For Missions.

ACORN Children's Publications, P.O. Box 11394, Lynchburg, VA 24506-1394. (804) 528-7840.

Curricula.
Shining Star Club Missionary Lesson Plans:
Devil-Kings and Cannibals.
George Mueller.
George Mueller Story/Pictures.
Hudson Taylor.
"I Dare."
Ly Huy's Escape.
Madugu.

New Life for Iromo, A.
No Darkness at All.
Praying Hyde.
Ringu.
Run, Ma Run.
Samuelito.

Fisherkids Club Missionary Lesson Plans:

Adventures in Brazil.
Devil-Kings and Cannibals.
"Go Ye."
"Go Ye" Story/Pictures.
Hudson Taylor.
"I Dare."
Ly Huy's Escape.
Nathan of Israel.
Praying Hyde.
Ringu.
Send Someone to Tell Me.
"So Send I You."

Stories.

George Mueller.
"Go Ye."
Gospel Ship Puppet Scripts.

Activities—Crafts, Activities and Decorations. **Activities and Crafts**.

Visual Aids. **Gospel Ship Puppet Scripts**.

Visual Aids—Flannel. **"So Send I You."**

Adopt-A-People Clearinghouse, P.O. Box 1895, Colorado Springs, CO 80901. (719) 473-8800.

Africa Evangelical Fellowship, P O Box 2896, Boone NC 28607. (704) 264-6036.

Books.

Child of Destiny.
Escape From the Darkness.
Mystery of the Scar.

Anatomical Chart Company, Skokie, IL. Order by phone: 1-800-621-7500.

Visual Aids—Posters. **People of the World**.

Angel's School Supply, 1987 Locust, Pasadena, CA 91107. (818)584-0855.

Visual Aids—Maps

Large Map

American Bible Society, 1865 Broadway, New York, NY 10023.

Bibles.

Arklings, The, Dept 9 ETC, 65300 Bend Redmond Hwy., Bend, OR 97701. (503) 389-3367.

Visual Aids—Puppets—Puppets and Supplies. **Catalog: Puppets, Patterns and Scripts**.

Augsburg Fortress, 426 S. Fifth Street, Box 1209, Minneapolis, MN 55440-1209. Publishers in other locations also. (612) 330-3300 or 1-800-328-4648.

Books.

Friends Around the World Series:

Friends in Asia.
Friends in Africa: A World Mission Activity Book.
Friends in Latin America.
Visiting in the Global Village, Volume 1 (El Salvador, Tanzania, Japan).
Visiting in the Global Village, Volume 2 (Indonesia, Cameroon, Brazil).
Visiting in the Global Villege, Volume 3 (India, Peru, Madagascar).

Baptist Book Store Mail Order Center, So. Baptist Convention, 127 Ninth Ave., North, Nashville TN 37234. On the West Coast send orders for materials to: 251 So. Randolph Ave., Brea, CA 92621. (714) 256-0277. Others call 1-800-233-1123 for orders or for one of 64 regional bookstores near you.

Curricula.

Indonesia: Islands of Flowers, Elephants, and Change Children's Packet.
Let's Go To India; 1992 Curriculum.
Worldtrek: 52 Missions Experiences for Children Grades 1-6.

Books—For Children.

Always a Friend.
Brown Eyes, Blue Eyes.
City: Sights, Sounds, and Smells, The.
Donald Orrs: Missionary Duet, The.
Dream Builders: The Story of the Forts of Africa, The.
Ed Taylor: Father of Migrant Missions.
Finlay and Julia Graham: Missionary Partners.
George Lozuks: Doers of the World, The
Harley Shields: Alaskan Missionaries, The.
It Was Always Africa.
Lady of Courage.
Lights, Camera, Love in Action.
Loyd Corder: Traveler for God.
Matthew's Dad is a Missionary.
Oz and Mary Quick: Taiwan Teammates.
Pattersons: Missionary Publishers, The
Shoemakes: God's Helpers, The.
Shoes On, Shoes Off.
Two Nichols: Spent For Mission, The.
Virginia Wingo: Teacher and Friend.
Who is a Missionary?
You Can be a Musician and a Missionary, Too.

Books—For Leaders. **How We Teach Missions in the Home.**

Stories.

My Mom and Dad Are Missionaries.
On the Big River.

Activities—Crafts, Activities and Decorations.
  Carousel of Countries, A.
  Fun Around the World.
  Guess What I Made!?!
  Mission Action Book, The.
  Worldtrek: 52 Missions Experiences for Children Greades 1-6.
Activities—Fund-Raising Projects. **Bank.** World Bank.
Activities—Games. **Missions Games and Activities for Children.**
Visual Aids—Maps. **World, Outline Map.**
Visual Aids—Posters and Pictures.
  Foreign Missions Preschool Pictures.
  Missions Pictures for Preschoolers.
Audio-Visuals—Cassettes and Records. **Mission Friends Cassette Tape.**
Audio-Visuals—Filmstrips.
  Many Faces of Korea, The.
  Nigeria, Home for Brian.

Baptist General Conference Board for World Missions (see also Harvest Publications), 2002 S. Arlington Heights Rd., Arlington Heights, IL 60005. (708)323-4215.

  Curricula—Youth. **Is This Missions Thing For Real?**

Baptist Mid-Missions , P.O. Box 308011. Cleveland, OH 44130. (216) 826-3930.
  Books.
    Flight from Death.
  Visual Aids. Flashcards.
    Abessende.
    Andrew and the Hurricane.
    Annie, Iowa Farm Girl.
    Big Storm, The.
    Clean Wash, A.
    Door that Opened, The.
    From Darkness to Light.
    Freedom from Fear.
    Gaston, The Love Servant.
    Living Word in Italy, The
    Madjou.
    Martiniana.
    On Wings of Song.
    Roberto.
    We Two Alone.
    Yangsan Starts a Church.

Beacon Hill Press of Kansas City, (see also Nazarene Publishing House or Children's Ministries/Div of SS Ministries), Box 419527, Kansas City, MO 64141.
  Curricula. **Mission Study Packet ('95)** (see Children's Ministries)

Bell, Janis, (see Kids Can Make a Difference)

Bethany House Publishers, 11300 Hampshire Ave. S., Minneapolis, MN 55438. (612) 829-2500. FAX: 612-829-2768.

> Books.

>> **Amy Carmichael.**
>> **The Trailblazer Series:**
>>> **Attack in the Rye Grass--Marcus and Narcissa Whitman.**
>>> **Bandit of Ashley Downs, The--George Mueller.**
>>> **Escape From the Slave Traders--David Livingstone.**
>>> **Flight of the Fugitives--Gladys Aylward.**
>>> **Hidden Jewel, The--Amy Carmichael.**
>>> **Imprisoned in the Golden City--Adoniram and Ann Judson.**
>>> **Shanghaied to China--Hudson Taylor.**
>>> **Trial by Poison--Mary Slessor.**

Bible League, The, Children Caring for Children Ministry, South Holland, IL 60473. 1-800-334-7017.

> Curricula, Activities—Projects, and Audio-Visuals—Videos. **Children Caring For Children**.

BGMC (Boys & Girls Missionary Crusade–AOG Churches, Sunday School Promotion and Training Dept., 1445 Boonville Ave., Springfield MO 65802.

> Curricula. Curriculum containing a children's missions education program used by and available from the Assemblies of God, for preschool and elementary children. A new packet is provided each quarter

BCM International, Inc., 237 Fairfield Ave., Upper Darby, PA 19082-2299. (215) 352-7177.

> Curricula and Visual Aids—Flannelgraph.
>> **Men God Used.**
>> **"So Send I You."**
>> **World Map** (Flannel).

> Books. **Yes Lord! What NOW?** (Available from the Division of BCM Youth Ministries, P.O. Box 268, Annville, PA 17003-0268.

> Visual Aids—Flashcards.
>> **Brother Andrew.**
>> **New Life for Iromo.**
>> **Tamenta.**
>> **Three Stories from India.**

> Audio Visual Aids—Slides. **"What Does God Want With A Kid Anyway?"** (Chet Bitterman)

Bible Memory Association, P.O. Box 12,000, Ringgold, LA 71068-2000. (318) 894-9154.

> Activities—Coloring books. **The Missionary Coloring Book.**

Bible True Audio Visuals, 144 S. Busse Rd., Mount Prospect, IL 60056. (312) 593-1454.

> Visual Aids—Puppets—Puppets. **Puppet Ministry Catalog**.

Bible Visuals, International, Box 153, Akron PA 17501-0153. (717) 859-1131.

> Visual Aids—Flashcards.
>> **A Chosen Friend.**

Antonio of Brazil/The Walking Umbrella.
Adventure in Brazil.
Doctor in the Pygmy Forest.
Doming the Popsicle Boy.
God's Bridge.
John and Betty Stam.
Ladi and White-White.
Laraba and Audu.
Ly Huy's Escape.
Miracle for Samuelito, A
Nathan Finds New Life in Jerusalem.
No Darkness At All.
Penny and the Christmas Star/How Turea Kept Christmas.
Praying Hyde.
Salvation and Sea Worms, A Story of Fiji.

Broadman Press, 127 Ninth Ave. N., Nashville, TN 37234. 1-800-251-3225.

Books. *Meet the Missionary Series:*
Caudills, The: Courageous Missionaries.
Donald Orrs, The: Missionary Duet.
Ed Taylor: Father of Migrant Missions.
Finley and Julia Graham: Missionary Partners.
George Lozuks, The: Doers of the Word.
Harley Shields, The: Alaskan Missionaries.
Hattie Gardner: Determined Adventurer.
John Allen Moores, The: Good News in War and Peace.
Loyd Corder, Traveller for God.
Oz and Mary Quick: Taiwan Teammates.
Pattersons, The: Missionary Publishers.
Shoemakers, The: God's Helpers.
Two Nichols, The: Spent for Missions.
Vena Aguillard: Woman of Faith.
Virginia Wingo: Teacher and Friend.

CAM International, 8625 LaPrada Dr., Dallas, TX 75228.

Activities—Crafts, Activities and Decorations. **Kid's World.**

Audio-Visuals—Slides, Videos. **Kids Can Be Missionaries Too.**

Center for Ministry to Muslims, 1315 Portland Ave. S., Minneapolis, MN 55404.

Activities—Coloring Books. **Color the Muslim World With Jesus' Love.**

Chalkboard, The, 2110 Plainfield Road (Rt 30), Joliet, IL 60435. (815) 741-2023; 1-800-688-6689.
Bulletin Boards, Decorations, Flash Cards, Games, Geography Activity Books, Maps (world and country), Ornaments, Story Cards, and much more. Request Catalog.

CHAMP (Children's Aspiring Missionary Program). Biblical Ministries Worldwide, 1595 Herrington Road, Lawrenceville, GA 30243-5616.

Activities—Newspapers (Leaders). **CHAMP** Program for Children.

Chariot/David C. Cook Publications, 20 Lincoln Ave., Elgin, IL 60120. (708) 741-0800.

    Books—**When I Grow Up, I Can Go Anywhere For Jesus.**

Child Evangelism Fellowship/CEF Press, Warrenton, MO 63383. (314) 456-4321. Orders: 1-800-748-7710.

    Curricula. **Special Ministries Kits:** Five-lesson kits each contain Bible lessons, Bible verses, missionary story, and visualized song.

        Children of the Bible Kit.
        Knowing Christ Kit.
        Lost and Found Kit.
        My Wonderful Lord Kit
        Strong In The Lord VBS Kit (1993).
        Wordless Book Visualized Kit.

    Activities—Magazines.
        Catalog.
        Evangelizing Today's Child.

    Visual Aids—Flannelgraph.
        Christian Soldier, The.
        Horizons Never End (Rochunga Pudaite).
        How the Dyaks Learned to Give.
        "I Dare." (Amy Carmichael: India).

    Visual Aids—Flashcards.
        Devil-Kings and Cannibals (John Paton: New Hebrides).
        His Best For God (Eric Liddell).
        Hudson Taylor (China).
        Madugu (Nigeria).
        Man for God's Plan, A (Jim Elliot: Ecuador).
        Mustapha's Secret (Morocco).
        Rejoicing With Joy (Joy Ridderhof).
        Ringu of India's Forest.
        Run, Ma, Run (Mary Slessor: Africa).
        Send Someone To Tell Me!
        Surrounded By Headhunters (Ecuador).
        Ti-Fam: Witch Doctor's Daughter (Haiti).
        Yandicu (Bolivia).

    Visual Aids—Posters and Pictures.
        Versatile Visuals for Salvation.
        Wordless Book.
        World's Children.

    Audio-Visuals—Videos.
        Bantu.
        Lion Territory.
        Pedro and the Bright City.

    Songs/Music—Source Books.
        Growing Songs For Children.
        Growing Songs For Children Cassette.

It's A Big, Big World. (Visualized Song)
Salvation Song Books #1-#4.

Children of Jesus Foundation, Inc., P.O. Box 31688, Palm Beach Gardens, FL 33420. (407) 790-2953. FAX 407-697-4864.

Activities—Magazines. **Children Vision International.** (for Leaders)

Children's Ministries/Div of S S Ministries/Nazarene Headquarters, 6401 The Paseo, Kansas City, MO 64131-1284. (816) 333-7000. FAX: (816) 333-4439. Note: Please call the publishing house (1-800-877-0777) before ordering for current themes and book titles and prices.

Curricula. **Mission Study Packet ('95)**containing five themes (see Curricula). A new Study Packet is published each year.

Books. **Adventures in Africa.** (call above number and request list of new books.)

Children's Mission Resource Center, U.S. Center for World Mission, 1605 Elizabeth, Pasadena, CA 91104. (818) 398-2474.

Curricula. **Children's Mission Sermons.**

Books—For Leaders.
    Junior High Curriculum.
    Kids for the World: A Guidebook to Children's Mission Resources.
    52 Fun Things Your Family Can Do Together for Missions.

Christian and Missionary Alliance Division of Church Ministries, 350 N. Highland Ave., Nyack, NY 10960.

Activities—Crafts, Activities and Decorations. **Taiwan Activity Book.**

Christian Education Commission, "George Fox Press" (see George Fox Press).

Christian Ed. Publishers, (see Rainbow Publishers)

Activities—Crafts, Activities and Decorations.
    52 Ways to Teach Children to Share the Gospel.
    52 Ways to Teach Missions.

Christian Literature Crusade, 701 Pennsylvania Ave., Box 1449, Fort Washington, PA 19034. (215) 542-1240.

Books.
ASHA'S ADVENTURES:
    (No.1) On the Trail of a Spy.
    (No. 2) Danger on the Sunita.
    (No. 3) The Red Gang.
    (No. 4) The Curse of the Amulet.
    (No. 5) Saved by Fire.
DEBBIE NEWTON SERIES:
    Ainesworth Prowler, The.
    House Beyond Congo Cross, The.
    Secret of the Old House, The.
BIOGRAPHIES:
    Ann H. Judson of Burma.
    Crusader for Christ.
    Doctor Who Never Gave Up, The.

Friend of the Chiefs.
From Slave Boy to Bishop.
God's Madcap.
Golden Foot.
Heroine of Newgate, The.
Knight of the Snows.
Millionaire for God.
Prophet of the Pacific.
Saint in the Slums.
South Seas Sailor.
Star Over Gobi.
White queen.
Wizard of the Great Lake.
Young Man in a Hurry.

Christian Publications, 3825 Hartzdale Dr., Camp Hill, PA 17011. (717) 761-7044. FAX: (717) 761-7273. To order toll free: (800) 233-4443.

Books.

The Junior Jaffray Collection; Missionary Biographies forChildren:
By An Unfamiliar Path.
Edge of Conflict.
Let My People Go.
Heart for Imbabura, A.
No Sacrifice Too Great.
On Call.
One Shall Chase a Thousand.
Please Leave Your Shoes at the Door.
To China and Back.
To Vietnam With Love.
"Weak Thing" in Moni Land.

Missionary - That's Me Series:
I Want to Be a Missionary.
Meet the Missionary.
Missing Missionary, The.
Missionary--That's Right.
Waiting Missionary, The.

Activities. 52 Ways to Teach Missions.

Stories. (in books)
Bare Beautiful Feet, and Other Missionary Stories for Children.
Happy Day for Ramona, A, and Other Missionary Stories for Children.
Pink and Green Church, The, and Other Missionary Stories for Children.
Potato Story, The, and Other Missionary Stories for Children.

Songs, Music—Musicals. M-I-S-S-I-O-N-A-R-Y That's Us!

Cities for Christ Worldwide, P.O. Box 300340, Escondido, CA 92030-0340. Contact Dr. Timothy & Dorothy Monsma. (619) 489-1812. FAX: 619-489-1813.

Activities—Projects. Street Kids Projects.

Compassion International, P O Box 7000, 3955 Cragwood Drive, Colorado Springs CO 80933. 719-594-9900.

>   Activities—Projects. **Compassion Projects.**

CB International (formerlyConservative Baptist Foreign Mission Society), P.O. Box 5, Wheaton, IL 60189-0005. (708) 665-1200. FAX (708)665-1418.

>   Curricula. **Missions Alive.**
>
>   Activities—Fund-Raising Projects.
>
>>   **Banks for Projects.**
>
>   Activities—Coloring Books.
>
>>   **Good News for the Chinese**
>
>   Visual Aids.
>
>>   **Flags, Placemats**
>
>   Audio-Visuals—Slides.
>
>>   **Kids Can be Missionaries Too.**

Conservative Baptist Home Mission Society, P.O. Box 828, Wheaton, IL 60189. (312) 653-4900.

>   Audio-Visuals—Film Strips. **Missionary Projects for Vacation Bible School**.

Constructive Playthings, 1227 East 119th Street, Grandview, MO 64030. 1-800-832-0572. Send for catalog.

>   Visual Aids—Globes. **Earth Globe** (Inflatable).
>
>   Activities—Decorations.
>
>>   **Children Around the World Wall Hanging.**
>>   **Christmas All Over the World.**
>>   **International Children Border.**
>
>   Activities—Games. **Friends Around the World Game.**

Cordova, Alice, 3535 13th Street, Vero Beach FL 32960.

>   Curricula. **Through Latin America**.

Crossroads Publications, P.O. Box 111475, Campbell, CA 95011. (408) 378-6658.

>   Curricula.
>
>>   **Escape By Night. (China)**
>>   **Trapped In Darkness. (Romania)**
>>   **The Secret Search. (Pakistan)**
>
>   Stories.
>
>>   **No Longer My Son–Malaysia.**
>>   **Nothing But Trouble–Guatemala.**
>>   **Snakes, Witch Doctors and Prayer–Liberia.**
>>   **Strange Encounter, A–India.**

Crosswalk Resources, 11000 E Washington Blvd., Whittier, CA 90606.

>   Activities. **My Missionary Friend Diary.**

David C. Cook Publishing Co., 850 N. Grove Ave., Elgin IL 60120. 1-800 - 437-4002.

>   Activities—Coloring Books. **Missionary Road and Color.**

Curricula. **Around the World With Jesus.**

Eerdmans, Wm. B., Publishing Co., 255 Jefferson Ave. S.E., Grand Rapids, MI 49503. (800) 253-7521.

Books. (Children Around the World books—see God's World Publications).

Esther Network, International, 854 Conniston Road, West Palm Beach, FL 33405-2131. (407) 832-6490. FAX: 407-832-8043. (Mail orders to: Karen Moran)

Books. **What About the Children?**

Activities—Crafts, Games.
How to Make a 10/40 Window Prayer Display.
Prayer Spinner.

Visual Aids—Globes. **"Globall."**

Songs, Music—Source Books and Audio Cassettes.
House of Prayer Sheet Music containing House of Prayer March and other 10/40 Window songs.
House of Prayer Cassette Tape with House of Prayer March and other 10/40 Window songs.

Evangelical Missionary Alliance, Whitefield House, 186 Kennington Park Road, London SE11 4BT, ENGLAND.

Every Child Ministries, Inc., P.O. Box 810, Hebron, IN 46341-0810.

Songs, Music—Source Books. **Easy-to-Learn Missionary Songs.**

Faith and Life Press, Box 347, Newton, KS 67114-0347. (800) 743-2484.

Curricula. **Neighbors Near and Far: Asians in Asia and North America**, and **Hispanic North America and Latin America**.

Books. **I Heard Good News Today.**

Family Book Center, 725 MacArthur Blvd., San Leandro, CA 94577.

Activities—Coloring Books. **Coloring Book About the Andes**.

Family Mission/Vision Enterprises, A division of Adleta Ministries, Inc., P.O. Box 7198, Bend, OR 97708-7198. Ph. (503) 317-1763. FAX (503) 317-1764. For Catalog information and orders: (800) 201-1668. Ask for newsletter/order form listing additional missions prayer, language and teaching tools.

Curricula. (espcially for home school use)
Teaching With God's Heart For the World, Volume I.
Teaching With God's Heart For the World, Volume 2.

Foreign Mission Board, Southern Baptist Convention Distribution Coordinator, P.O. Box 6767, Richmond, VA 23230-9970.

Books.
John and Julie Go to Japan.
Kazuko's Family.
Yakubu.

Audio-Visuals—Videos. **School Someday.**

Fox, George, Press. See George Fox Press.

Friends of Turkey. 508 Fruitvale Ct., Grand Junction, CO 81504.

>   Activities— Projects.

>> **Be a Missionary At Home!**
>> **Be a Pen-Pal and Share the Gospel!**

Friendship Press, 475 Riverside Dr., New York, NY 10115.

>   Curricula.

>> **Aki and the Banner of Names.**
>> **Aki and the Banner of Names (Teachers' Guide).**
>> **Choices and Other Stories. (Teachers' Guide).**
>> **Courage For a Cross.**
>> **Courage For a Cross (Teachers' Guide).**
>> **Crickets and Corn.**
>> **Mi Jun's Difficult Decision.**
>> **Pearl Makers.**
>> **Pearl Makers (Teachers' Guide).**
>> **Won Gil's Secret Diary.**

>   Stories.

>> **Choices and Other Stories form the Caribbean.**
>> **World of Children's Stories, A.**

>   Activities.

>> **Children's World Series.**
>> **Listen To a Shadow.**

>   Activities—Games. **A World of Children's Games.**

>   Activities—Newsletters. **Follow the Sun.**

>   Songs—Books. **A World of Children's Songs.**

Frontier Fellowship/Global Prayer Digest Orders, 1605 Elizabeth Street, Pasadena CA 91104. (818) 398-2249.

>   Stories—**The Global Prayer Digest.**

Frontiers, (or Frontiers Associates) 325 North Stapley Drive, Mesa, AZ 85203. (602) 834-1500. For orders only: 1-800 GO-2-THEM. FAX 602 834-1974.

>   Curricula. **Destination 2000 A.D.**

>   Activities—Projects. **10 Practical Ways For Kids .....**

General Conference Mennonite Church, Commission on Education, Box 347, Newton, KS 67114. (316) 283-5100, FAX: (316) 283-0454.

>   Curricula.

>> **Neighbors Near and Far: Africans and Black Americans.**
>> **Neighbors Near and Far: Asians in Asia and North America.**
>> **Neighbors Near and Far: Hispanic north America and Latin America.**
>> **Neighbors Near and Far: Native People in North America.**

Geography Placemats. Dept. MP-168, 1145 North Ellis Street, Bensenville, IL 60106.

>   Visual Aids—Maps. **World Map Placemats.**

George Fox Press, Christian Education Commission, Evang. Friends Int, N A Region, 110 S Elliott Rd., Newberg, OR 97132. (503) 538-9775. FAX: 503-538-7033.

Books.

Catching Their Talk in a Box.
Down a Winding Road.
From Here to There and Back Again.
Happiness Under the Indian Trees.
Keeping Them All in Stitches.
Mud on Their Wheels.
No Time Out.
Outside Doctor On Call.
What Will Tomorrow Bring?
Whistling Bombs and Bumpy Trains.

God's 4 Kid's, c/o Singing for Jesus Ministry, 704 Leaming Avenue, North Cape May, NJ 08204. (609) 886-9253.

Books. **God's 4 Kid's Book Club**.

Stories—Newsletters. **"GOD'S 4 KIDS."**

God's World Publications, (God's World Books), P.O. Box 2330, Asheville, NC 28802. For Credit card orders, call   1-800-951-BOOK.

Books.

A Boy's War. (David Mitchell)
Nothing Daunted. (Isobel Kuhn)
With Daring Faith: A Biography of Amy Carmichael.

Visual Aids—Atlas. **Atlas of the World.**

Good Apple, Inc., Box 299, Carthage, IL 62321. (217) 357-3981.

Activities. Crafts, Activities and Decorations.
More Windows to the World.
Windows to the World.

Good News Productions, International, P.O. Box 222, Joplin, MO 64802-0222. (417) 782-0060.

Curricula. Also Projects, and Audio-Visuals—Videos.
Days of Discovery.

Gospel Films, Box 455, Muskegon, MI 49443-0455.

Audio-Visuals—Videos. **Peace Child.**

Gospel Light/Regal Publications, P.O. Box 3875, Ventura, CA 93006. (805) 644-9721. For orders only, 1-800-4-GOSPEL.

Activities. Crafts, Activities and Projects.
(Contained in VBS and Churchtime programs.)

Visual Aids—Maps. **World Missions Map.**

Visual Aids—Puppets. **Easy-to-Make Puppets and How to Use Them.**

Audio-Visuals—Cassettes, Records.
Missionary Adventure Stories, Tape 1.
Missionary Adventure Stories, Tape 2.

Gospel Missionary Union, 10000 N. Oak, Kansas City, MO 64155.
> Curricula. Visual Aids—Flashcards.
>> **Mustapha's Secret.**
>> **Surrounded By Headhunters.**
>> **Yandicu.**

Harvest Publications, 2002 S. Arlington Heights Rd., Arlington Heights, IL 60005. For orders: (800) 323-4215.
> Curricula. **Is This Missions Thing for Real?** (for High Schoolers)

HCJB World Radio, P.O. Box 39800, Colorado Springs, CO 80949-9800. (719) 590-9800. FAX: (719) 590-9801. (Also called World Radio Missionary Fellowship, Inc.)
> Activities—Projects. **VBS Missions Projects.**
>
> Visual Aids—Flashcards. **HCJB, Shortwave Goes a Long Way.**

Heifer Project International, P.O. Box 808, Little Rock AR 72203. 8 other regional offices in the United States.
> Curricula—also Activities—Projects. **Animal Crackers.**

Highlands Community Church, 3031 NE Tenth, Renton, WA 98056. Attn: Karen McCabe, Co-ordinator. 206-255-4751. FAX: (206) 255-5460.
> Curricula. **Kinderclub Curriculum** (ten packets for Kindergarten). **"God Loves...."**
>> **The Philippines, Alaska (Natives), Africa, Japan, Our Samaria, Me!, Thankful People, Germany, Israel, and South America.**
>> **KWAM! (Kids With A Mission!—first to sixth grades).**

Hope Publishing House, P.O. Box 60008, Pasadena, CA 91116-1331. (818) 792-6123; FAX (818) 792-2121. (see also William Carey Library)
> Books.
>> **Mission Adventures In Many Lands.**
>> **Mission Stories From Around the World.**

Institute of Chinese Studies, 1605 Elizabeth St., Pasadena, CA 91104. (818) 398-2320.
> Curricula. **Taiwan's Urban Working Peoples.**
>
> Books and Activities—Coloring books. **Drawn to China.**
>
> Visual Aids—Maps. **China.**

International Bible Society, P.O. Box 35700, Colorado Springs, CO 80935-3570. Call 1-800-524-1588 with VISA or Master Card Ordrs. Or call Robert Swales at (719) 488-9200.
> **Bibles and New Testaments.**

International Films. P.O. Box 40400, Pasadena, CA 91104. (818) 797-5462.
> Audio-Visuals—Films.
>> **Humpty.**
>> **Last Out, The.**
>> **Little Lost Fisherman.**
>> **Mysterious Book.**
>> **Tanglewood Secret.**
>> **Treasures in the Snow.**
>
> Audio-Visuals. Video. **Humpty**

<u>Iranian Christians International Inc.</u>, P O Box 2415, Ann Arbor MI 48106.

Books. **Tales of Persia.**

<u>JAARS, Inc.</u>, P.O. Box 248, Waxhaw, NC 28173. (704)843-6000. FAX (704)843-6200.

Activities—Coloring Books. **Fly Beyond the Mountain.**

<u>Kaleidoscope,</u> 11314 Woodley Ave., Granada Hills, CA 91344. (818) 831-1927.

Books, Leaders. **Catalog.**

Visuals Aids, Flannel, Globes, Puppets.

> **Children of the World (felt).**
> **Families on Felt. (Black family, Hispanic family, Oriental family, and Caucasian family)**
> **Forever Friends—Pretty Pals (flannel)**
> **Stick Puppets.**

Activities, Decorations. **Globe key rings.**

<u>Kids Can Make A Difference</u> (see Bell, Jan), 4445 Webster Dr., York, PA 17402. Tel. & FAX (717) 757-6793.

Curricula.

> **Around the World With Jesus.**
> **Feed My People.**
> **Festival of Faith.**
> **Let's Explore Missions; Adventures in the Far East.**
> **Passport to Adventure.**
> **Which Way to God?**

Books—For Children.

> **All Paths Lead To Bethlehem.**
> **Christmas Around the World.**
> **Communicating The Christmas Story Cross-Culturally.**
> **Culturgrams: Vol. 1 and Vol. 2.**
> **Joy to the World.**
> **Kwanzaa.**
> **Man Who Would Not Hate, The**
> **People Book.**
> **Question of Yams, A.**
> **Then and Now: The CIS States.** Series includes **Armenia, Azerbaijan, Belarus, Estonia, Georgia, Kazakhstan, Latvia, Lithuania, Moldoa, Russia, Tajikestan, Turkmenistan, Ukraine, Uzbekistan.**
> **TRAILBLAZER SERIES, THE: David Livingstone, William & Catherine Booth, Martin Luther, John Wesley, Amy Carmichael, William Tyndale, Adoniram and Ann Judson, George Muller, Mary Slessor, Hudson Taylor, Marcus & Narcissa Whitman.**

Books—For Leaders. **Bi-annual Catalog.**

Stories.

> **Lost in the Rain Forest.** (also in Games)
> **Sound of the Bell, The.**
> **Story of Ana, The.**

Activities—Coloring Books. **Missionaries Coloring Book, The.**

Activities—Fund-Raising Projects. **Read-to-Feed.**

Activities—Crafts, Activities, Decorations and Games.

Arabs: Activities for Elementary School Level, The.
Best Board Games From Around the World.
Color the Muslim World With Jesus' Love.
Count Your Way.
Embrace Your World.
Ethnic Celebrations Around the World.
Faces of the Watching World.
Fun Around the World.
Guess What I Made.
Kidscan Packet.
Lost in the Rain Forest.
My Missionary Friend's Diary.
"P-Words."

Visuals Aids, Flannel. **Children of the World.**

Audio-Visuals.

Audio tape. **The Kuta Story—An Indonesian Miracle.**

Videos.

Carlos of Columbia.
First Valentine, The.
Kambari
KIDSCAN Video.
Malay Kids.
Operation Coconut.
Patna Kids.
Sugarcane Island.

Songs—Music—Cassette Tapes and/or Songbooks.

Charlie Cherub; Go Into All the World.
I Am a House of Prayer.

Lakeland Bible Mission, Inc., 3205 Kiess Rd., Bucyrus, OH 44820-9636. (419) 562-6471.

Curricula.

Children's Missionary Conferences.
Is a Missionary? #1.
What Does A Missionary Do? #3.
Witness-Servant-Chosen #2.

Songs—Books. **Missionary Chorus Books.**

Lakeland Child Evangelism Ministries, Inc., P O Box 612, Winona Lake IN 46590. (219) 594-5344.

Audio-Visuals—Videos.

Hidden Island.
Rescue In Manila.

Also have videos in Spanish.

Lakeshore Learning Materials, 2695 E. Dominguez Street, Carson, CA 90749. 1-800-421-5354.

Visual Aids—Posters. **Children of the World Poster Pack.**

Lerner Publications, 241 First Ave. N., Minneapolis, MN 55401.

Books. **Family in...** series.

Lutheran Bible Translators,303 N Lake Street, Box 2050, Aurora IL 60507-2050. (708)897-0660. or 1-800-53-BIBLE. FAX: (708) 897-3567. Materials FREE, but donations appreciated.

Activities—Coloring Books/Sheets.
God's Word For Us and Others.

Activities—Banks, Crafts, Maps.
African Village House Bank.
Language Project Maps.
Lord's Prayer in the Krio Language, The.
Mission Lesson & Crossword Puzzle.
Mission Lesson & Hidden Word Puzzle.
Mission Scene Coloring Sheet.
Psalm 23 in the Atikamekw Language.
Teacher's Guide.
Translation Samples.

Audio-Visuals—Videos.
And It Was Good Soup!
With Their Own Eyes.
Word Has Arrived, The.

Maher, Dept TC, Box 420, Littleton, CO 80160. (303) 798-6830. FAX: (303) 798-3160

Visual Aids—Puppets—Puppets and Supplies. **Catalog: Puppets and Supplies for Ventriloquist\Puppet Ministry.**

Mission to the World (Presbyterian Church in America), Box 1744, Decatur, GA 30031.

Stories. **Children's Mission Stories.**

Mission Vision Network (a ministry of Far East Broadcasting Company), Box 1, La Mirada, CA 90637.

Audio-Visuals--Cassettes. **A World of Praise.**

Missions Education, P.O. Box 2337, Anderson, IN 46018.

Curricula.
Adventures in Peru and Bolivia.
An American Child Visits Japan.
Arabic Adventure.
Crickets and Corn.
I Am Important.
It Happened in Bolivia.
Land Along the Nile.
My Friends in India.
Our Amigos In America.
Our Friend Kee Yazzie.

Trip to the Land of the Rising Sun, A.
Welcome To India.

Missionary Aviation Fellowship, Attn: Gloria Graham, P.O. Box 3202, Redlands, CA 92373-0998. (714) 794-1151, Ext. 247, or FAX: 714-794-3016.

Curricula and Videos.

Flights For Kids
Flights for Kids Video.

Activities—Coloring Books/Sheets.

MAF Helps People.

Missionary Church Inc., Dept. of Children's Ministries, 3901 So. Wayne Ave., Fort Wayne IN 46807.

Activities—Newsletters. **Acorn'r Missionary Newsletter for Children.**

MLB Designs, (Mary Lou Bohnsack White), Mission America 2000, 901 E. 78th Street, Minneapolis, MN 55420-1300. (612) 853-1743.

Visual Aids—Puppets.

Individual Puppets: African, Eskimo, Mexican, Muslim, Polynesian, each with a story.
Unreached People Group Puppets: Tribal, Hindu, Chinese, Muslim, Buddhist, each with a story.

Monarch Publishing, Bev Gundersen, 245 Second Ave. NE, Milaca, MN 56353. (612) 983-2398.

Curricula. **WORLD FOCUS Books:**
Complete Set (or):
World Focus, Leader's Guide.
World Focus, Tribal People Groups, Mexico, Grade 1.
World Focus, Chinese People Groups, China, Grade 2.
World Focus, Buddhist People Groups, Japan, Grade 3.
World Focus, Muslim People Groups, Indonisia, Grade 4.
World Focus, Hindu People Groups, India, Grade 5.
World Focus, World Christians, Grade 6.
GLOBAL NIEGHBORS --- Series:
Meet the Navajos.
Native North Americans.
Paulo and the Earthquake.
Stories.
Missions and Me
Activities. Crafts, Activities and Decorations. **WINDOW SERIES Activity Books: Window to Alaska, Window to Mexico, Window to Japan, Window to Germany, Window to the C.I.S., Window to Kenya, Window to Korea, Window to Pakistan, Window to India, and Window to Zaire.**
Jesus Loves the Children of the World
Native Americans Calendar
World Children Calendar.

Activities—Coloring Books/Sheets.
> **Great Global Activities.**
> **Jesus Loves the Children of the World.**
> **Muslim Factivities.**

Activities—Games. **Great Global Games.**

Navajo Missions, Inc., Farmington, NM.

Activities—Coloring Books. **Indian Children's Missionary Stories.**

Nazarene Publishing House, (see also Beacon Hill Press of Kansas City), P.O. Box 419527, Kansas City MO 64141.

New Hope Publishing (WMU), P.O.Box 12065, Birmingham, AL 35202-2065. (205) 991-4933.

Books.
> **Doña Maria & Friends.**
> **Lady of Courage: The Story of Lottie Moon.**
> **Mission Stories For Young Children.**

Activities—Crafts, Activities and Decorations.
> **Carousel of Countries, A**
> **Fun Around the World.**

NWMS (Nazarene Mission Study) (see also Beacon Hill Press), 2923 Troost, Kansas City MO 64141.

OM LIT, P.O. Box 28, 129 Southside Drive, Waynesboro, GA 30830. For credit card book orders, call toll free 1-800-733-5907

Books.
> **Around the World With Logos.**
> **Jim Elliot, Missionary to the Rain Forest.**

Activities. **You Can Change the World Activity Books** (Book One and Two).

Visual Aids—Maps. **Pray For the World;** Hammond World Map.

OMF Books, 10 West Dry Creek Circle, Littleton, CO 80120-4413. Bookline: 800-422-5330.

Curricula. **Back Home in Japan** (Teacher's Guide and Student Book).

Books.
> **Jeff Anderson Series:**
>> No. #1. **East Into Yesterday.**
>> No. #2. **East of the Misty Mountains.**
>> No. #3. **East To the Shifting Sands.**
> **Ai-Chan's Secret.**
> **Before the Moon Dies.**
> **Boy's War, A.**
> **Broto.**
> **Gods Must Be Angry, The.**
> **Granny Han's Breakfast.**
> **Hudson Taylor, Trusting God.**
> **Ian and the Gigantic Leafy Obstacle.**
> **Kim and Ting.**
> **Loompy–Mission Dog.**

Maki's Busy Week.
My Book About Hudson.
New Toes for Tia.
Nid's Exciting Day.
Back Home in Japan (student book). (See Curricula.)
Let's Look at...(Indonesia, Malaysia, Philippines, Thailand) Series.

Visual Aids—Flashcards.
Faun and the Naughtiest Pig/Boy from Mindoro.
Seiko and the Spider's Thread.
Young Ki's Courage/Sold Twice.

Audio-Visuals—Videos.

Children's Missionary Stories: contains the three former slide stories above, **Before the Moon Dies, How "Mr. Don't-Feel-Like It" Lost His Name,** and **Ian and the Gigantic Leafy Obstacle.**

One Way Street, Inc., Box 2398, Littleton, CO 80161. (303) 790-1188. Orders only: (800) 569-4537. FAX: (303) 790-2159.

Curriculum.
Around the World With Jesus.
Junior Missionary Retreat.

Activities.
52 Ways to Teach Missions.
Junior Missionary Retreat.

Activities—Skits, Drama. **Skituations "The Missionary."**

Visual Aids—Puppets—Puppets and Supplies.
Catalog: Puppet Ministry.
Easy-to-Make Puppets.
Puppet Scripts on Missions.

Visual Aids Songs, Music—Musicals. **Kids Praise 6** (Tape and Songbook).

Oriental Trading Company, P.O. Box 3407, Omaha, NE 68103-0407. 1-800-228-2269. Send for catalog.

Visual Aids—Globes.
Earth Squeeze Balls.
Metal Globe Key Chains.
"Our Earth" slide puzzles.
Plastic Earth Glide Balls.

Overseas Crusades (OC Ministries, Inc.), 25 Corning Ave., Milpitas, CA 95035-5336. (408) 263-1101.

Write missions curriculum for the children of their staff.

Partners International, P.O. Box 15025, San Jose, CA 95115-0025. (408)453-3800. FAX: (408) 437-9708.

Activities—Fund-Raising Projects.
Projects to Choose from Through Partners International.

Activities. Crafts, Activities and Decorations. **Passports.**

Pasadena Map Co., 2341 Foothill Blvd., Pasadena, CA 91107. (818) 795-3626.

Globes of all sizes and colors (rigid, stuffed and inflatable). Maps of all shapes, sizes and colors (world and country), umbrella world maps, and map jackets.

Pioneer Clubs/Pioneer Ministries, Box 788, Wheaton, IL 60189-0788. (708)293-1600. FAX 1-800 619-CLUB or (708) 293-3053.

Books — Leaders. **Making Missions Meaningful.**

Puppet Pals, 6686 Lee St., Arvada, CO 80004.

Visual Aids—Puppets—Puppets and Supplies. **Brochure/Price List: Puppets, Patterns, Scripts, other materials.** Write for free brochure.

Visual Aids—Puppets—Books/Printed Materials. **Instruction Books.**

Puppet Productions, Inc., P.O. Box 82008, San Diego, CA 92138. (619) 565-2343.

Visual Aids—Puppets—Puppets and Supplies. **Catalog: Puppets and Supplies.**

Quadrangle/The New York Times Book Co., 330 Madison Ave., New York, NY 10017.

Songs/Music—Source Books. **Sing, Children, Sing.**

RAF Ministries Inc., (Richard Farmer) 100 Ross St., Pittsburgh PA 15219.

Songs/Music—Source Books--Cassettes.

This is Missions; and Seven Other Missions Songs.

Rainbow Books/Christian Ed. Publishers, P.O. Box 261129, San Diego, CA 92196-9980. For orders only: 1 (800) 854-1531.

Activities—Crafts, Activities, and Decorations.
52 Ways to Teach Children to Share the Gospel.
52 Ways to Teach Missions.

Randall House Publications, P.O. Box 17306, 114 Bush Road, Nashville TN 37217. For orders (800) 877-7030, (615) 361-1221.

Curricula and Visual Aids—Flashcards. **Missionary Stories About....**

R.C. Law & Co., 579 S. State College, Fullerton, CA 92631. (800) 777-5292.

Curricula. **Mini-Missions Conference for Children.**

Reber, Christopher, 312 N. Main Street, Topton, PA 19562.

Visual Aids—Maps. **Map Placemat.**

Reformed Church Press Distribution Center, 3000 Ivanrest SW, Grandville, MI 49418. Phone 800-688-7221.

Activities—**Children, Let Us Love! Every Fifth Child in the U.S. Faces Hunger.**

Sacred Literature Ministries, Inc., P.O. Box 777, Taylors, SC 29687. (803)244-7524.

Books and Activities—Crafts, Decorations, Projects. **Missions Ideas.**

Activities—Newsletters. **Teacher's Swap Shop.**

Scripture Press Publications, Inc., 1825 College Ave., Wheaton, IL 60187. 1-800-323-9409 or (312) 668-6000. (See Victor Books/SP Publications, Inc.)

Curricula.

Children's Church Primary Programs (One each, 1989, 1990 & 1991).
Junior Teaching Resources Packet (1991).

Visual Aids—Puppets. **Six animal hand puppets.**

SIM USA, P.O. Box 7900, Charlotte, NC 28217. (704)588-4300.

Curricula. **What in the World are Missions?**

Books—For Children.

Adventures of Tonko.
Never Hide a Hyena in a Sack.
Rat-Catcher's Son, The.
Rick-a-Chee... Series.
Secret of the Forest Hut.
Snake Stories from Africa.
Stories from Africa.

Audio-Visuals—Cassettes and Records.
Snake Stories from Africa.
Stories from Africa.

Audio-Visuals—Videos. All the **Rick-a-Chee** books listed above, two stories per video.

SKITuations, P.O. Box 773 Corona, CA 91718. (800) 322-1336.

Activities—Skits, Dramas. **"The Missionary"** Vol. XIV.

TEAM, P.O. Box 969, Wheaton, IL 60189-0969. (708) 653-5300.

Books.

Bobby In Japan.

Activities—Coloring Books. **France Coloring Book.**

Trans World Radio, International Headquarters, Attn: Rosemarie Jaszka, PR Director, P.O. Box 8700, 300 Gregson Drive, Cary, NC 27512-8700. (919)460-3700. FAX: 919-460-3702.

Activities—Coloring Sheets.
Escape to the Jungle.
Reaching Brazil by Radio.
Reaching the World By Missionary Radio.

Audio-Visuals—Cassettes. **Kids Talk.**

Activities—Newsletters. **Radio Kids!**

UNICEF, 1 Children's Blvd., P.O. Box 182233, Chattanooga, TN 37422. Available from: (in Calif.) United Nations Ass'n.–USA, Pasadena Chap. Inc., 723 E. Green St., Pasadena CA 91101. (818)449-1795. Or write or call: U.S. Committee for UNICEF, 333 East 38th Street, New York NY 10016. (212)686-5522. Also request the latest catalog.

Activities—Games. **Games of the World.**

Visual Aids—Pictures. **Desk Calendar, (1996).**

Visual Aids—Globes. **Hugg-A-Planet, Earth.**

Universal Four, 423 South Blvd., Oak Park IL 60302. (800) 423-5686.

    Books. **Ethnic Pride.**

University of the Nations, School Primary Health Care, 75-5851 Kuakini Hwy, Kailua-Kona, HI 96740-2199. (808) 326-7228, FAX: (808) 329-2387. Ask for Rosemary Rinker.

    Curricula—**Building Your Temple.**

U.S. Center for World Mission, 1605 Elizabeth St., Pasadena, CA 91104l (818)797-1111. Mission Resource Center: (818)398-2236. Children's Missions Resource Center: (818)398-2233. Frontier Fellowship (for **Global Prayer Digest** and **Mission Frontiers** magazine orders): (818) 398-2249.

U.S. Flag Supply, Inc., 101 Bridge Street, Rt 3A, North Weymouth, MA 02191. For orders, call 1-800-444-8504, FAX 800-452-3366.

    Visual Aids—Flags. **U.S. Flags, State Flags, Custom Banners, Foreign Flags, and more in many sizes.**

Victor Books/SP Publications, Inc., 1825 College Ave., Wheaton, IL 60187. (312) 668-6000. (See Scripture Press Publications).

    Books—For Leaders.

        Youth and Missions: Expanding Your Students' World View.

    Activities (also Books—For Leaders). **Reach Around the World.**

Warren's Educational Supplies, 7715 Garvey Ave., Rosemead, CA 91770. (818)966-1731.

    Visual Aids—Maps. **Maps, all sizes**

    Books—**Crafts of Many Cultures**

WEC International Media Dept., P.O. Box 1707, Fort Washington, PA 19034-8707. Or call (215) 646-2322.

    Books.

        Colombian Jungle Escape.
        Operation World.
        You Can Change the World.

    Visual Aids—Flashcards. **Charles Studd.**

    Audio-Visuals—Slides.

        Amy and Nicole.
        Carlos of Colombia.
        Gaga of Zaire.
        Mussa of North Africa.
        Som Chai of Thailand.
        That Others May Hear.

    Audio-Visuals—Video.

        Each of the above, or

        Six Stories from WEC (all on one video).

    Stories, and Activities—Crafts, Activities and Decorations. **Kiddie Leaflets** (on 25 different countries).

Westlake Bible Church, Children's Ministries Department, 3423 Bee Cave Road, Austin TX 78746.

> Curricula. **Missions Units.**

William Carey Library, P.O. Box 40129, Pasadena, CA 91114. (818) 798-0819; Orders: (800) 777-6371.

> Books.
>> **Broto.**
>> **From Arapesh to Zuni.**
>> **Gods Must Be Angry, The,**
>> **Granny Han's Breakfast.**
>> **Mission Adventures in Many Lands.**
>> **Mission Stories From Around the World.**
>> **My Book About Hudson.**
>> **Nid's ExcitingDay.**
>> **Peace Child.**
>> **What Language Does God Speak?**
>> **When I Grow Up I Can Go Anywhere For Jesus.**
>> **You Can Change the World.**
>
> Books for Leaders:
>> **Catalog (call for latest).**
>> **Operation World.**
>
> Activities—Crafts, Activities, Projects, Games. **Missions Made Fun For Kids.**
>
> Activities—Coloring. **You Can Change The World Coloring Books**; Two-Book Set.
>
> Visual Aids—Map. **Bibles For All Map.**
>
> Visual Aids. Posters and Pictures. **Unreached Peoples 1990.**
>
>> Audio-Visuals—Videos.
>>> **God's Kaleidoscope.**
>>> **Peace Child.**

Word, Inc., 4800 West Waco Dr., Waco TX 76796.

> Music—Musicals. **Heart To Change the World.**

World Changers Resources, P.O. Box 830010, Birmingham, AL 35283-0010. (205) 991-4933.

> Books for Leaders, and Activities.
>> **Missions Alive.**
>> **Missions Games and Activities For Youth.**

World Vision, 919 W. Huntington Dr., Monrovia, Ca 91016. (818) 357-7979, ext. 2528. For the Project listed, call (818) 357-1111, ext. 3437.

> Activities—Fund Raising Projects. **What Can 1 Person Do?**

Worldfriends Press, P.O. Box 830010, Birmingham, AL 35283-0010. (Publishes Missions MatchFile for Children by Brotherhood Commission, SBC, and WMU, SBC, jointly.)

> Curricula.
>
>> **Missions MatchFile Kits.**
>
>> **WorldTrek; 52 Missions Esperiences for Children Grades 1-6.** (Also in Activities)

<u>Wycliffe Bible Translators</u>, P.O. Box 2727, Huntington Beach, CA 92647 (714) 969-4600.

Books.

Danger in the Blue Lagoon/Din Be Still.
From Arapesh to Zuni.
Night of the Long Knives.
When I Grow Up, I Can Go Anywhere for Jesus.

Activities—Coloring Books, Brochures, and Coloring Sheets.

Can You Guess Brochure.
Children's Language Brochure.
What Language Does God Speak?

Audio-Visuals—Slides. **What Language Does God Speak?**

Audio-Visuals—Video. **God's Kaleidoscope**.

10

Index of Missionaries

(Materials Dealing with Specific Missionaries)

Aguillard, Vena
   Books. **Vena Aguillard: Woman of Faith**.

Allison, J. D. R.
   Books. (Leader's). **Great Missionaries in a Great Work**.

Andrew, "Brother"
   Visual Aids—Flashcards. **Brother Andrew, God's Smuggler**.

Annan, Robert
   Books. **God Made Them Great**.

Aylward, Gladys
   Books. **Flight of the Fugitives**. (Story of Gladys Aylward—Trailblazer Books)

Becker, Dr. Carl
   Visual Aids—Flashcards. **Doctor in the Pygmy Forest**.

Bollback, Anthony and Evelyn Bollback
   Books. **To China and Back**.

Brainerd, David
   Books. **God Made Them Great**.
   Visual Aid—Flannel. **So Send I You**.

Bray, Billie
   Books. **God Made Them Great**.

Cable, Mildred
   Books. **Star Over Gobi**.

Carmichael, Amy
   Curricula. **"I Dare."** (also with lesson plans)
   Books. **Amy Carmichael**.

      God's Madcap.

      Hidden Jewel, The. (Story of Amy Carmichael—Trailblazer Books)

Let the Little Children Come to Me; Amy Carmichael.

With Daring Faith: A Biography of Amy Carmichael.

Visual Aids. Flannelgraph. **"I Dare."**

Carey, William

Curricula. **Children's Church Primary Program (1992)**

Books. **Great Missionaries in a Great Work** (Leader's).

Young Man in a Hurry.

Carlson, Millie (see Resource Persons)

Former missionary in Venezuela, now working with her husband Daryl as regional representatives for the Evangelical Free Church/America missions program.

Cattell, Catherine

Books. **Happiness Under the Indian Trees.**

Caudills, The

Books. **Caudills, The: Courageous Missionaries.**

Choate, Ralph and Esther

Books. **What Will Tomorrow Bring?**

Corder, L.

Books. **L. Corder, Traveller for God.**

Cordova, Alice (see Resource Persons)

Missionary, writer, who wrote **Through Latin America.**

Columbus, Christopher

Curricula. **Children's Missions Sermons** (Christopher Columbus).

Couture, Eugene (see Resource Persons)

Missionary, writer, speaker, and co-author of children's missions curricula.

Crowther, Samuel Adjai

Books. **From Slave Boy to Bishop.**

Custer, Geraldine

Books. **Keeping Them All In Stitches.**

Cutts, Bill and Grace

Books. **Weak Thing in Moni Land.**

DeVol, Dr. Ezra and Frances

Books. **Outside Doctor On Call.**

Devol, Charles

Books. **From Here to There and Back Again.**

Driskill, Lawrence (see Resource Persons)

Former missionary, writer of children's missionary stories and books.

Drown, Frank and Marie
Curricula. **Surrounded By Headhunters.**

Dulka, Ed and Doreen
Books. **Colombian Jungle Escape.**

Elliot, Jim
Visual Aid—Flashcard. **Man for God's Plan, A.**

Ellis, Vern and Lois
Books. **Mud on Their Wheels.**

Finley, Ruth (see Resource Persons)
Former missionary, writer of missions curricula, speaker.

Fort, Giles and Wana Ann
Books. **The Dream Builders: The Story of the Forts of Africa.**

Francis, Mabel
Books. **One Shall Chase a Thousand**
Books (Leader's). **Great Missionaries in a Great Work.**

Fry, Elizabeth
Books. **Heroine of Newgate, The.**

Gardner, Hattie
Books. **Hattie Gardner: Determined Adventurer.**

Graham, Billy
Books. **Crusader for Christ.**

Graham, Finley and Julia
Books. **Finley and Julia Graham: Missionary Partners.**

Grenfell, Wilfred
Books. **Knight of the Snows.**

Harms, Dr. David
Books. **Dr. Harms, the Helper.**

Harrell, Mrs. Marguerite, M.Ed. (see Resource Persons)
Former missionary, teacher, writer of curriculum, **Developing World Christians.**

Hege, Ruth and Irene Ferrl
Visual Aids—Flashcards. **We Two Alone.**

Hibschman, Barbara
Speaker, former Missionary, Author, Teacher. Author of over 200 articles and poems, and 8 books (see Resource Persons).

Hyde, John (Praying Hyde)
Curricula, and Visual Aids—Flashcard. **Praying Hyde** (also with lesson plans).

Ilnisky, Esther

> Founder of Esther Network International, which seeks a million child intercessors to pray for Unreached Peoples in the "10/40 Window." She heads up the children's department for the AD2000 & Beyond United Prayer Track. Wife of a missionary/pastor (see Resource Persons).

Jaffray, Robert

> Books. **Let My People Go.**
>
> Books (Leader's). **Great Missionaries in a Great Work.**

Judson, Adoniram

> Books. **Adoniram Judson.** (2)
>
> > **Golden Foot** (and Ann Judson).
> >
> > > **Imprisoned in the Golden City -- Adoniram Judson.**
>
> Books (Leader's). **Great Missionaries in a Great Work.**
>
> Visual Aid—Flannel. **So Send I You.**

Judson, Ann

> Books. **Ann H. Judson of Burma.**

Kagawa, Toyohiko

> Books. **Saint in the Slums**

Kievngere, Festo (of Uganda)

> Books. **The Man Who Would Not Hate.**

Kimber, Sandra (England)

> Former missionary, wrote the resource book, **WORM**, now has a ministry called CHIME Worldwide. CHIME stands for CHildren In Mission and Evangelism (see Resource Persons).

Klaus, Sandy

> Missionary, writer of children's materials with Gospel Missionary Union (see Resource Persons).

Knight, Roscoe and Tina

> Books. **Down a Winding Road.**

Kuhn, Isobel

> Books. **God Made Them Great.**

Land, Mitchell and Family

> Stories. **My Mom and Dad Are Missionaries**.

Liddell, Eric

> Books. **Eric Liddell.**
>
> Visual Aids—Flashcards. **His Best For God**.

Livingstone, David

> Books. **Escape From the Slave Traders(Story of David Livingstone - Trailblazer Books).**

Books (Leader's). **David Livingstone.**
 Great Missionaries in a Great Work.

Lozuk, George

Books. **George Lozuks, The: Doers of the Word.**

Lull, Raymond

Visual Aid—Flannel. **So Send I You.**

Mackay, Alexander

Books. **Wizard of the Great Lake.**

McWhorter, Mildred

Books. **Always a Friend.**

Mission Aviation Fellowship Missionaries (various)

Curricula, and Audio-Visual Aids—Videos. **Flights For Kids.**

Mitchell, David

Books. **A Boy's War.**

Moffat, Robert

Books. **Friend of the Chiefs**

Monsma, Dr. Tim and Dorothy

The Monsmas are directors of Cities For Christ Worldwide, former missionaries in Africa, and direct the outreach trips, for and with children (see Resource Persons).

Moody, Barbara

Missionary (sent on research trip to Uzbekistan), writer of "Uzbek Curriculum" (see Resource Persons).

Moon, Lottie

Books. **Lady of Courage: The Story of Lottie Moon.**

Moore, John Allen

Books. **John Allen Moores, The: Good News in War and Peace.**

Mueller, George

Curricula, and Stories. **George Mueller (also with lesson plans).**
Books. **God Made Them Great.**
 The Bandit of Askley Downs (Story of George Mueller—Trailblazer Books).
Stories. **George Mueller.**

Nichols, The

Books. **Two Nichols, The: Spent for Missions.**

Nixon, Anna

Books. **Whistling Bombs and Bumpy Trains.**

Orr, Donald

Books. **Donald Orrs, The: Missionary Duet.**

Pate, Mavis

Books. **Clothed in White.**

Paton, John G.

Curriculum and Flashcards. **Devil-Kings and Cannibals** (with lesson plans).
Books. **Prophet of the Pacific.**

Patrick, St.

Curricula. **Children's Missions Sermons** (St. Patrick).
Visual Aid—Flannel. **So Send I You.**

Pattersons, The

Books. **Pattersons, The: Missionary Publishers.**

Peters, David and Arlene

Books. **By An Unfamiliar Path.**

Pressly, Sarah

Has written **Back Packing: 2000 B.C. to 2000 A.D.,** a book for pre-teens about Bible-time "back-packers," who resembled modern day Pakistani people. Former missionary to Pakistan (see Resource Persons).

Presswood, Ernest and Ruth

Books. **No Sacrifice Too Great.**

Pudaite, Rochunda

Visual Aids—Flannelgraph. **Horizons Never End.**

Richardson, Don

Books, and Audio-Visuals—Video. **Peace Child.**

Quick, Oz and Mary

Books. **Oz and Mary Quick: Taiwan Teammates.**

Ridderhof, Joy

Books. **Catching Their Talk in a Box.**
Visual Aid—Flashcard. **Rejoicing With Joy.**

Rychner, Evelyn

Books. **Heart for Imbabura, A.**

Sahlberg, Corrine and Elmer

Books. **Please Leave Your Shoes at the Door.**

Scaggs, Josephine

Books. **It Was Always Africa.**

Schultz, Dorothy

Curricula. **Mini-Missions Conference for Children.** Missionary/teacher in Papua New Guinea, speaker, resource person. Founded Children's Missions Resource Center. (see Resource Persons).

Scudder, Ida

    Books. **Doctor Who Never Gave Up, The.**

Shetler, Jo

    Activities—Coloring Books. **What Language Does God Speak?**
    Audio-Visuals—Slides. **What Language Does God Speak?**

Shields, Harley

    Books. **Harley Shields, The: Alaskan Missionaries**.

Shoemakers, The

    Books. **Shoemakers, The: God's Helpers.**

Skinner, William and Frances

    Books. **Two Dreams and a Promise.**

Slessor, Mary

    Curricula, and Visual Aid --Flashcard. **Run, Ma, Run.**
    Books.

        White Queen .
        Trial By Poison (Story of Mary Slessor—Trailblazer Books).

Sperger, Babbi

    Missionary, mobilizer, teacher, speaker and singer. Co-director with her husband of the Latin American Center for World Mission. Records Spanish song and story tapes (see Resource Persons).

Stam, John and Betty

    Visual Aids—Flashcards. **John and Betty Stam.**

Studd, C.T.

    Books. **Millionaire for God.**
    Stories. **Charles Studd.**
    Visual Aids—Flashcards. **Charles Studd**.

Swan, Dr. William

    Books. **Matthew's Dad is a Missionary.**

Taylor, Ed

    Books. **Ed Taylor: Father of Migrant Missions**.

Taylor, Harry and Miriam

    Books. **Edge of Conflict.**

Taylor, Hudson

    Curricula. **Children's Church Primary Programs** (1992)
        Hudson Taylor (also with lesson plans).
    Books.

        Hudson Taylor, Trusting God.
        J. Hudson Taylor: For God and China.

> **My Book About Hudson.**
> **On the Clouds to China: The Story of Hudson Taylor.**
> **Shanghaied to China** (Story of Hudson Taylor - Trailblazer Books).

Books (Leader's). **Great Missionaries in a Great Work.**

Flashcard. **Hudson Taylor.**

Theriault, Judy

Teacher, speaker, coordinator of Perspectives courses, and writer of children's missions curricula, and adult's missions articles. Gone on missions outreaches, and is co-director of the Presbyterian Center for Mission Studies (see Resource Persons).

Thomas, George and Dorothy

Books. **No Time Out.**

Thompson, David

Books. **On Call.**

Tichy, Nancy

Former missionary, co-ordinator of Perspectives courses, teacher, workshop speaker, writing and editing poetry, writing for magazines, and writer of children's missions materials (see Resource Persons).

Tinder, Edie,

Missionary to Belgium, teacher, writer (see Resource Persons).

Williams, John

Books. **South Seas Sailor.**

Wingo, Virginia

Books. **Virginia Wingo: Teacher and Friend.**

Winter, Roberta (see Resource Persons).

Former missionary to Guatemala, Assistant Executive Director, USCWM, speaker, author.

Whitman, Marcus and Narcissa

Books. **Attack in the Rye Grass** (Story of Marcus and Narcissa Whitman—Trailblazer Books).

Ziervogel, Jim, Institute of Chinese Studies (see Resource Persons).

Former missionary to China, writer, speaker, director of Institute of Chinese Studies, and author of *Drawn to China* and *Taiwan's Urban Working Peoples.*

Zinzendorf, Count

Visual Aid—Flannel. **So Send I You.**

Note: <u>MAF missionaries</u> are featured in the curriculum **Flights For Kids.**

11

Children's Mission Education Resource Persons

<u>Alley, Steve and Cora,</u> Children's Church, Inc., P.O. Box 773, Corona, CA 91720. (714) 737-8969.

College professors, authors of *SKITuations* series books.

<u>Amos, Joyce Anna,</u> Missionary Action Great Lakes, 1824 E. First Street, Duluth, MN 55812.

Assistant Director of Missionary Action, resouce person, speaker, chrildren's teacher and Mobilizer to the Latin American church.

<u>Andrews, Joyce,</u> World Mission Prayer League, Inc., 232 Clifton Ave., Minneapolis MN 55403. (612) 871-6843.
Resource person.

<u>Apgar, Sue,</u> Wycliffe Bible Translators Inc., P O Box 2727, Huntington Beach CA 92647. (714) 969-4630. Home: (714) 969-1853.

Sue has developed two dramas depicting the entrance of the gospel into the language and culture of the Chipaya Indians of Bolivia's Altiplano and the Quechua Indians of Ayacucho, Peru. Given monologue style, she is available mostly in Southern California for churches, Sunday Schools, Christian schools, and mission conferences. They are geared mostly for junior age on up through adults.

<u>Bashta, Dick and Susie,</u> P.O. Drawer AA, Reserve, LA 70084. Contact them at (504) 536-4506 or (504) 652-1436.

Dick is field representative for Gulf States Missions Agency. Susie writes and produces missions drama, does speaking, and shares children's missions ideas. They have mission field experience and are available to assist churches.

<u>Bell, Janis,</u> Kids Can Make a Difference, 4445 Webster Dr., York, PA 17402. (717) 757-6793.

Writer, publisher, speaker, resource person. See Publishers index.

<u>Bohnsack White, Mary Lou,</u> MLB DESIGNS, Mission America 2000, 901 E. 78th Street, Minneapolis, MN 55420-1300. (612) 853-1743.

Speaker and resource person, missions education specialist, makes and distributes Finger Puppets.

<u>Bradford, Dr. John and Kathy,</u> 2620 Glen Drive, Missoula, MT 59801. (406) 721-7751.

Founders and directors of "World Missions Forum." In cooperation with ACMC and YWAM, they sponsor area-wide missions conferences and workshops, with a strong emphasis on children.

Brown, Audrey, 2048 Westlawn Dr., Kettering, OH 45440. (513) 434-4524.

Missions education specialist for "The Alliance World," a publication of Christian publications; and missions writer for several publications.

Brown, Judy, 620 Paxton Ave., Loveland, OH 45140. (513) 683-3553.

Writer of Children's Church Missions Curricula for Grace Brethren Churches.

Cadonau, Anita, c/o Beaverton Foursquare Church, 13565 S W Walker Road, Beaverton, OR 97005.

Children's ministry director, workshop speaker, and writer of Curriculum. Call (503) 644-2801, to order *Children of the World Travel Agency* Curriculum.

Campbell, Barbara, c/o ACMC, P.O. Box ACMC, Wheaton, IL 60189-8000. (708) 260-1660.

Missions Education resource person, speaker, and author of the book, *I Don't Want To Wait Until I'm Grown Up.* , and *Who Is A Missionary?* Curriculum.

Carlson, Millie, 1732 Fairacre Drive, Greeley, CO 80631. (303) 353-9204.

Former missionary in Venezuela, now working with her husband Daryl as regional representatives for the Evangelical Free Church/America Missions program. Has a children's missions resource center in her home especially for Evangelical Free Churches in their region, speaks in churches and missions groups. Has co-authored a missions curriculum especially for Evangelical Free Churches.

Cordova, Alice, 3535 13th Street, Vero Beach, FL 32960.

Missionary, writer. Wrote *Through Latin America.*

Couture, Eugene, Lakeland Bible Mission, Inc., 3205 Kiess Rd., Bucyrus, OH 44820-9636. (419) 562-6471.

Missionary, writer, speaker.

Driskill, Lawrence, Hope Publishing House, P.O. Box 60008, Pasadena CA 91116. (818) 792-6123.

Former missionary, writer of children's missionary stories and books.

Dueck, Gerry, Children's Mission Resource Center, USCWM, 1605 Elizabeth, Pasadena, CA 91104. (818) 398-2233; (818) 797-0595; or (818) 398-2232 (leave message).

Resource person, director of Children's Mission Resource Center. Compiled *Kids for the World.*

Dunagan, Ann, 21589 Bear Creek Road, Bend, OR 97702; or P.O. Box 6326, Bend, OR 97708. Ph (503) 389-4380.

Educator, home school mother, pastor/evangelist's wife, writer, speaker, and co-founder (with her husband) of Harvest Ministry (an international evangelistic outreach ministry), and founder of Family Mission/Vision Enterprises (the publishing arm). Wrote 2 missions-centered home school curricula, *Teaching With God's Heart For the World, Volume 1,* and *Volume 2.* (see Curricula)

Finley, Ruth, 1290 S. Baywood Ave., San Jose, CA 95128. (408) 248-4321.

Missionary, writer, speaker. Assisted in writing *Escape by Night* , *Trapped in Darkness.*, The Secret Search, INDIA–A Strange Encounter, LIBERIA–Snakes, Witch Doctors and Prayer, MALAYSIA–No Longer My Son, and GUATEMALA–Nothing But Trouble.

Gorke, Nancy, Church on the Way, 14300 Sherman Way, Van Nuys, CA 91405.

Christian education director, workshop leader, resource person.

Graham, Gloria, Flights For Kids Coordinator, MAF, P.O. Box 3202, Redlands, CA 92373-0998. (714) 794-1151.

Author and coordinator of children's material.

Griffo, Paul and Marcy, White Fields, P.O. Box 45173, Washington, DC 20026-5173.

Writers and publishers of the Newsletter "White Fields," a children's missionary newsletter.

Gundersen, Bev, Monarch Publishing , 245 Second Ave. NE, Milaca, MN 56353. (612) 983-2398.

Author, publisher, author of "Window" series, WORLD FOCUS Curriculum., and other missions materials.

Hanson, Alberta, Ph D., 21056 Multnomah Road, Apple Valley CA 92308. (619) 247-7834.

Educator, teacher, speaker, and missions activist for many years. Also has a resource center in her home.

Harrell, Mrs. Marguerite, M.Ed., 875 N W 13th Street Apt. 315, Boca Raton, FL 33486. (407) 395-2420.

Former missionary, teacher, writer of curriculum "Developing World Christians," teaches missions to children in Christian day school.

Harris, Gregg, Christian Life Workshop, 180 S E Kane Road, Gresham, OR 97080.

Teaches missions to children as well as adults, using the book *Operation World.*.

Harris, Jill, FRONTIERS, 325 N. Stapley Drive, Mesa, AZ 85203. (602) 834-1500.

Children's missions education specialist, speaker, mobilizer, and co-developer of the "Destination 2000" curriculum for children.

Hibschman, Barbara, 95 DockWatch Hollow Road, Warren, NJ 07059-6910. (908) 560-0910.

Speaker, former missionary, author, teacher. Author of over 200 articles and poems, and 8 books.

Hockett, Betty, 1100 N. Meridian #38, Newberg, OR 97132. (503) 538-9871.

She is a speaker, curriculum writer, and author of the "Life Story From Missions Series" books for children (there are now 9). Alternate address: 18303 SE River Rd., Portland, OR 97267.

Ilnisky, Esther, Esther Network International, 854 Conniston Road, West Palm Beach, FL 33405-2131. (407) 832-6490. FAX: (407) 832-8043.

Speaker andfounder of the Network which seeks a million child intercessors to pray for unreached peoples in the "10/40 Window." She heads up the children's department for the AD2000 & Beyond United Prayer Track.

Kimber, Sandra, 11a Upper Teddington Road, Hampton Wick, Kingston-upon Thames, Surrey, KT1 4DL U K.

Former missionary, teacher, speaker to missionary organizations and churches in the U.K., motivates missions, youth, and children, provides resources for the task to be done. Was with EMA Youth Ministries, but now has a new ministry called CHIME Worldwide.

CHIME stands for Children In Mission and Evangelism, and will involve a club and magazine to give children a world mission view.

Klaus, Sandy, 203 S. Garfield, Oblong, IL 62449.

Missionary, writer with Gospel Missionary Union.

Kordik, Mary Ellen, 9605 West Ruby Ave., Wauwatosa, WI 53225.

Available for workshops, member of missions committee in her church.

Loftin, Laurie Eve, P.O. Box 632, Glen Ellyn, IL 60138.

Writer, speaker, and missions education specialist. Has compiled an "Annotated Bibliography of Resources for Contemporary Missions Education and Cultural Awareness." See Books for Leaders.

Middleton, Barth and Sally, CEF teacher training directors for the state of Michigan.

Seminar speakers, writers, and teacher trainers for CEF. Wrote article "Can I Prepare Children for Overseas Ministry?" for *Evangelizing Today's Child*, CEF's publication.

Monsma, Dr. Tim and Dorothy, Cities For Christ Worldwide, P.O. Box 300340, Escondido, CA 92030-0340. (619) 489-1812. FAX: (619) 489-1813.

The Monsmas are directors of the above agency, former missionaries, and direct the outreach trips.

Moody, Barbara, c/o Caleb Project, 10 W. Dry Creek Circle, Littleton, CO 80120-4413.

Missionary, writer of Uzbek curriculum.

Parrott, Ele, (missionary now in Argentina).

Teacher, curriculum developer, resource person, author of *Kinderclub* Missions packets.

Partrich, Gretchen, 604 King St., Chadron, NE 69337.

Director of Children's Mission Education for the Church of the Nazarene in Nebraska.

Paul, Betty, 1246 N. Altadena Dr., Pasadena, CA 91107. (818) 798-4301.

Writer, teacher, (now retired) composer of Curriculum for Christian Day School. Author/composer of song *Far Away*.

Piper, Noel, c/o Bethlehem Baptist Church, 720 - 13th Ave South, Minneapolis MN 55415.

Speaker for workshops, and missions education resource person.

Pressly, Sarah, P.O. Box 92, Duke West, SC 29639.

Former missionary to Pakistan, writer of book **Back Packing; 2000 B.C. to 2000 A.D.**, a book for pre-teens about Bible time "back-packers," who resembled modern-day Pakistani people.

Rino, Dorothy, God's 4 Kids, c/o Singing for Jesus Ministry, 704 Leaming Ave., N. Cape May, NJ 08204. (609) 886-9253.

Publishes the bulletin "God's 4 Kids," a mail-order service especially for home-schoolers, and sponsors projects that donate food and clothes to poor children.

Roberts, Jackie, 2631 Beethoven, Portage, MI 49002. (616) 327-2338.

Resource person, speaker, writer.

Robertson, Karen. Now a missionary teacher in Indonesia.

Teacher, author of "Children's Mission Sermons" and co-author with Bev Gundersen of WORLD FOCUS Curriculum, and other people group materials for children.

Schultz, Dorothy, 2328 Primrose St., Eugene, OR 97402.

Missionary teacher in Papua New Guinea, teacher, speaker, resource person. Founded Children's Missions Resource Center. Author of *Mini-Missions Conference for Children*..

Schwarm, Dennis, 1734 Barton, Eugene, OR 97404.

Children's missions teacher, promoter and use of missions materials.

Schorr, Shari, c/o Antioch Alliance Church, 11947 Antioch Road, Logan OH 43138.

Children's church director, missions committee member and missions mobilizer.

Smith, Patti. United World Mission, Box 8000, St. Petersburg, FL 33738.

Missions speaker and children's teacher.

Snyder, Eleanor, 57 Stirling Avenue North, Kitchener, ON N2H 3G4, CANADA. (519) 745-9025.

Writer, educator, and director of Children's Education for the Commission on Education of the General Conference Mennonite Church.

Sperger, Babbi, Apdo. 1307-1000, San Jose, COSTA RICA.

Is a mobilizer, teacher, speaker and singer. Co-director with her husband of the Latin American Center for World Mission. Records Spanish song and story tapes.

Spiegel, Julie, CEF worker in Michigan.

Teacher, speaker, starts children's missions clubs as an outgrowth of "Good News" Clubs.

Templeton, Geri, Calvary Chapel, 1010 Tustin, Santa Ana, CA 92705.

Christian Education/Children's Ministries director, speaker, writer, resource person. Featured speaker in children's ministry workshops at ACMC.

Theriault, Judy, Presbyterian Center for Mission Studies, 1605 Elizabeth Street, Pasadena, CA 91104.

Teacher, speaker, and writer of children's missions curricula, and adult's missions articles.

Tichy, Nancy, 1600 S. San Jacinto #44, San Jacinto, CA 92583. (909) 654-3007.

Former missionary, co-ordinator of Perspectives courses, teacher, workshop speaker, writing and editing poetry, writing for magazines, and writer of children's missions materials. Write her for missions stories she has written.

Tinder, Edie, St. Jansbergstng 97, 3030 Leuven, BELGIUM.

Missionary, teacher, writer.

Villegas, Henry A., MD, FAAP, Children of Jesus Foundation, Inc., P.O. Box 31688, Palm Beach Gardens, FL 33420. (407) 790-2953. FAX: 407-697-4864.

President and C.E.O. of CJF, director of Health and Social Affairs of CJF, publisher of *Children Vision International* magazine, pediatrician, organizes mission trips to San Jose, Costa Rica, to set up a children's ministry there, conducts workshops and exhibits at missions and other conferences.

Wanner, Janet, 1466 Kennebec Road, Grand Blanc, MI 48439.

Janet and her husband are both experienced ministers. She is also a mission education resource person, writer, speaker, consultant, and workshop leader.

Weiner, Robert, Maranatha Campus Ministries International, P.O. Box 1799, Fainesville, FL 32602. (904) 375-6000

President of above agency which ministers to international students in the U.S. and other countries. Speaker, and writer of the book *Friend of God..* Assists children to start their own children's missionary society.

Welch, E. SIM, P.O. Box 7900, Charlotte NC 28241.

Former Missionary, wrote the original booklet "52 Fun Things Your Family Can Do Together For Missions."

Wilcox, Conrad H., TEAM Missions Education Consultant, 318 Clinton Court, Wheaton, IL 60187. (312) 665-1903.

Former missionary, resource contact, speaker for seminars and workshops.

Winter, Roberta, 1605 Elizabeth St., Pasadena, CA 91104. (818) 398-2230.

Missionary, Assistant Executive Director, USCWM, speaker, author.

Yeagle, Linda, c/o U.S. Center for World Mission, 1605 Elizabeth St., Pasadena, CA 91104.

Teacher, writer, speaker, developer of children's materials.

York, Mark, 6401 The Paseo, Kansas City, MO 64131.

Author, editor of Children's Mission Education Curriculum for Beacon Hill Press, promotes children's mission education in his church.

Ziervogel, Jim, Institute of Chinese Studies, 1605 Elizabeth St., Pasadena, CA 91104. (818) 398-2320.

Missionary, writer, speaker, director of Institute of Chinese Studies, and author of *Drawn to China* and *Taiwan's Urban Working Peoples.*

PART II

SAMPLES

12

CURRICULAR OUTLINES

The following are samples of weekly lesson plans, most of which the author has actually used in teaching grades Kindergarten through 6. Two Christmas and one Easter lessons are included. Some general observations and suggestions:

—Pictures, posters, maps, slides, videos, puppets or other visual aids should be used in each lesson.

—Illustrate all the songs whenever possible with pictures, and large colorful lettering, printing the words on tagboard; or use overheads.

—Use games, snacks, activity tables, additional songs as desired. Be creative, and use other activities as appropriate.

—Use missionaries whenever they are available, and switch lessons accordingly.

—You may choose to use either term: "Hidden" or "Unreached People Groups."

—Always close in prayer, encouraging children to volunteer to pray for the specific people group or country featured in the lesson.

Lesson 1: Unreached People Groups.

(For Pre-School–Grade 1, use Pre-School Introductory Lesson on pages II-13-14.)

Use complete Introductory Lesson to Hidden Peoples (p. II-15) for grades 1-6. Use world globe; posters for five major people groups; hand or paper bag puppets featuring children of various countries or areas. Include Burma Plan Story, if time.

Song: "Jesus Loves the Little Children." (Use red, yellow, black and white colored paper as suggested in Songs section.)

Activity: Color picture of children on Hidden Peoples page. Use as finger puppets if desired (see picture in Activities section).

Prayer: for all Hidden Peoples.

Lesson 2: Bible Translations/Bibleless People Groups.

Story: "What Language Does God speak?" (from WCL or Wycliffe).

Visual Aid: Choose one or more of the pictures in the book for overhead or coloring page. Bring your English Bible and a Bible in another language, if possible, to illustrate story. You may rent the slide show which coordinates with the book, from Wycliff. Call them to reserve it.

Songs: "Children of A 1,000 Tongues" (*Salvation Song Book #2*, p. 24) and "Jesus Died For

All the Children" (Tune: "Jesus Loves the Little Children").

Activity: Reproduce one of the pictures from the book, one for each child to color.

Prayer: for Hidden People Groups in the Philippines.

Lesson 3: Make Disciples of All Nations.

Story: "Good News Bus" (from set of "Five Children's Missions Sermons," by Karen Robertson. Available from CMRC).

Visual Aid: Make a large yellow bus from tagboard, following directions in story. Optional: world map.

Songs: "Children of A 1,000 Tongues." Learn "Good News" (*Growing Songs*, p.46; may purchase the illustrated song from CEF. Substitute the word "ALL" for "I' and "me."

Activity: As suggested in lesson.

Prayer: for Hidden Peoples all over the world, use globe or map.

Lesson 4: Unwilling Missionary.

Story: "Christopher Columbus" (from "Five Children's Missions Sermons").

Visual Aid: Bring a world globe or map to illustrate where Columbus went. The activities also provide the visual aids.

Songs: "Jesus Loves Them," as suggested in the story (tune: "Jesus Loves Me"), and review "Good News."

Activity: Use activities suggested in the lesson, making boats.

Prayer: for missionaries to go to Hidden People Groups.

Lesson 5: All Nations/Peoples.

Story: "Building God's House" (from "Five Children's Missions Sermons").

Visual Aid: Make picture of a house on tagboard, paste small velcro strips in many places all over the house, and bring small pictures of people from various people groups, pasting the other velcro strips on the backs of them (see suggestions in story). Have children participate in attaching the people on and in the house as you teach the story. Also, bring a tool box or bag with tools, as suggested in the story.

Songs: "We Can Build God's House," as suggested in lesson (to tune of "Row, Row, Row Your Boat"), and "All the Children Ought to Know" (*Savation Song Book* #4, p.2).

Activity: Use activities from the story.

Prayer: for all Unreached People Groups.

Lesson 6: Christ Died For All Peoples.

(appropriate for Easter or the week before Easter)

Story: "Lift High the Cross" (from "Five Children's Missions Sermons").

VisualAid: Make cross as suggested in the story.

Songs: "Jesus Died For All the Children" (see Lesson 2), and "Jesus Loves the Unreached Children" (both to tune of "Jesus Loves the Little Children," see Songs Section).

Activity: Do activity suggested in lesson.

Prayer: For all Unreached Peoples to come to Jesus.

Lesson 7: Good News For All Peoples.

Story: "St. Patrick" (from "Five Children's Missions Sermons").

Visual Aid: Find pictures of St. Patrick, and use visuals from story.

Songs: "Jesus Loves the Unreached Children" and "Jesus Rose For All the Children" (tune "Jesus Loves the Little Children").

Activity: Use activity sheets in the story.

Prayer: For more missionaries to go to Unreached Peoples.

Story: "Heaven and Sin"; combine Lesson 5 and 6, and use Lessons 1 and 2 from "Visualized Wordless Book" from CEF.

Visual Aid: "Wordless Book," and word sheets "Heaven and Sin."

Songs: "Wordless Book" song (*Salvation Song Book* #2, p. 10) and "Nzambi Ke Mbote."

Activity: Draw picture of heaven or sin. May play game: Heaven game from Lesson 5.

Memory Verse: John 14:2 (copies of verse from book; omit v. 3).

Prayer: for all the children of the world.

Lesson 8: Muslim People Groups.

Story: "Mussa of North Africa" (from WEC, see Videos). Rent or purchase the six-story video.

Activity (and visual aid): Have a Middle-East-type bazaar of several "shops" with snacks—olives, dates, cheeses, dried apricots, and other finger foods—for the children to purchase using play money. Teach them to barter for their purchases. Use a separate table for each "shop."

Songs: "All the Children Ought to Know," "Hari Ini," or others learned in previous lessons.

Prayer: for the Muslims of North Africa.

Lesson 9: Radio Broadcasting to ALL Languages.

Story: "HCJB" flashcard story.

Visual Aid: the flashcard story.

Songs: Learn "Young Folks, Old Folks" (*Salvation Song Book* #4, p. 79), and review "Good News."

Activity: Bring tape recorder and have children do role-playing with recording and then listening. They may record Bible verses, or any messages they would want to share with someone about God's love for ALL peoples.

Prayer: for Unreached Peoples in ALL countries to hear the Good News on gospel radio.

Lesson 10: Who Is A Missionary?

Story: Combine Lesson 1 and 2 from the curriculum *Who Is A Missionary* (from ACMC). You need not use all 11 lessons; choose which ones, or combine lessons. Teach and use the other stories in future lessons. "The Seed and the Soil," from the "Parables of Christ" (from CEF).

Visual Aids: Video: "Kids Can Be Missionaries Too" (from CAM).

Songs: Learn "Stop–Go–Watch" (*Growing Songs*, p. 42), and "All the Children Ought To Know."

Activity: Draw picture from Lesson 1 or play game from Lesson 2.

Memory Verse: Luke 24:47 (make copies from book).

Prayer: for all the tribal peoples in Africa.

Lesson 11: Love and Care for Others (from "Who Is A Missionary?")

Story: The "Good Samaritan" from the "Parables of Christ" (see Lesson 10).

Visual Aids: Use ideas from Lessons 3 and 4 in *Who Is A Missionary?*

Songs: "Stop–Go–Watch" (see Lesson 10), and learn "John 3:16" to the tune of "Silent Night" for Christmas (see Songs section).

Activity: Use game suggestions from the book, or draw picture from the lesson.

Memory Verse: Matthew 22:39b (make copies from book).

Prayer: for all the Buddhist people groups.

Lesson 12: Who Is A Missionary?

Memory Verse: II Timothy 2:15; use verse sheet from the lesson.

Songs: Learn "Little Missionaries" (*Salvation Song Book* #2, p. 22), and review "Good News."

Activity: Draw picture of what the child would to do to be a missionary. Play "Hangman to learn the memory verse.

Prayer: for all the Chinese Unreached People Groups.

Lesson 13: CHRISTMAS Lesson.

Story: "Communicating the Christmas Story Cross-Culturally." A Christmas lesson by Jan Bell. Shorten it and adapt to your missionary(from Kids Can Make A Difference).

Visual Aid: List of words, "P" words, an orange, and items suggested in lesson.

Songs: "John 3:16" (see Lesson 11), and other Christmas songs. Might rehearse all songs learned so far, to present them in a Christmas program.

Activity: As suggested in the lesson.

Prayer: for the missionary you are studying, and the people among whom he works.

Lesson 14: Tribal People Groups.

Story: "Gaga of Zaire" (from WEC video).

Visual Aid: Video.

Songs: "John 3:16," andlearn "Nzambi Ke Mbote" (Kituba language, Zaire; tune, "God Is So Good"; see Songs).

Activity: Idea: make and/or decorate Christmas cookies to take to a shut-in, plus one for each child.

Prayer: for children in all the tribal people groups around the world to hear about Jesus this Christmas.

Lesson 15: Who Is A Missionary?

Story: "Jesus' Blood and Witnessing." Combine Lesson 7 and 8; and Lesson 3 and 4 from "Wordless Book."

Visual Aid: "Wordless Book" and word sheets saying Blood and New Life.

Songs: "Wordless Book" song (see Lesson 12), and "Good News" (see Lesson 3).

Activity: Eat an ethnic snack food.

Memory Verse: Acts 4:20 (use verse sheet from book).

Prayer: for the missionaries from your church.

Lesson 16: Who Is A Missionary.

Story: Combine Lessons 9 and 10, using "The Talents" from "Parables of Christ" flashcard stories.

Visual Aid: Flashcards with the Parables story.

Visual Aid: "Wodless Book," and word sheets "Heaven and Sin.

Lesson 17: Buddhist People Groups.

Story: Show video "Som Chai of Thailand" (from WEC video), or order video and coordinated lesson plan from Kids Can Make A Difference.

Visual Aid: Video.

Songs: "Waga Shu Iesu" (Japanese for "Yes, Jesus Loves Me"; see Songs section) and first verse and chorus of "Bring Them In" (*Salvation Song Book* #1, p. 64).

Activity: Weave mats of 9"x12" contruction paper, resembling sleeping mats in Thailand.

Prayer: for the Buddhist peoples in Thailand.

Lesson 18: Tribal Peoples of Columbia.

Story: "Carlos of Columbia," a video with coordinated lesson plan to order from Kids Can Make A Difference.

Visual Aid: Bring artifacts from Columbia.

Songs: Learn "Cristo Me Ama" (see Songs section) and use "Wordless Book" song.

Activity: Prepare and eat soft flour tortillas; prepare fillings of meat, lettuce and cheese and have children make their own.

Prayer: for all the tribal peoples in Columbia.

Lesson 19: Bible Translation.

Story: *What Language Does God Speak?* slide program. Order book and slides from Wycliffe in advance (see Coloring books, and Audio-Visuals—Slides section).

Visual Aid: Slide show "What Language Does God Speak" (rent or buy from Wycliffe).

Songs: Use a song in a foreign language (see Songs section) and "Wordless Book" song.

Activity: Color a page from *What Language Does God Speak?* coloring book.

Prayer: for all the children in the Balangao Group.

Lesson 20: Story of Amy Carmichael.

Story: "I Dare," Part I. (See Visual Aids—Flannelgraph section.) Order and use "I Dare" from CEF Press and the supplementary curriculum book from ACORN Children's Publications (see Publishers).

Visual Aid: Flannelgraph figures from story "I Dare".

Songs: "I Have Decided to Follow Jesus" (*Salvation Song Book* #4, p. 76) and "Little Missionaries" (see Lesson 16).

Activity: Use lesson plans, crafts, and songs from the "I Dare" activity book.

Prayer: for hidden peoples in India.

Lesson 21: Story of Amy Carmichael.

Story: "I Dare," Part II.

Visual Aid: Flannelgraph figures from story "I Dare."

Songs: "I Have Decided to Follow Jesus" and songs from the activity book.

Activity: Use lesson plans and crafts from the activity book.

Prayer: for all the children in India.

Lesson 22: Story of Amy Carmichael.

Story: "I Dare," Part III.

Visual Aid: Flannelgraph figures from story "I Dare".

Songs: "Little Missionaries" (see Lesson 16) and learn "Far Away," stanza 1 (see Songs).

Activity: Use lesson plans and crafts from the activity book.

Prayer: for the evangelists and preachers in India.

Lesson 23: Story of Amy Carmichael.

Story: "I Dare," Part IV.

Visual Aid: Flannelgraph figures from story "I Dare."

Songs: "Far Away" (Stanzas 1 and 2), and "I Have Decided to Follow Jesus."

Activity: Use lesson plans and crafts from the activity book.

Prayer: for the many people groups in India.

Lesson 24: Story of Amy Carmichael.

Story: "I Dare," Part V.

Visual Aid: Flannelgraph figures from story "I Dare."

Songs: "Little Missionaries" and all 3 stanzas of "Far Away."

Activity: Use lesson plans and crafts from the activity book.

Prayer: for all missionaries in India.

Lesson 25: Muslim People Groups--Indonesia.

Story: Lessons 1 and 2 from World Focus book, Muslim People Groups—Indonesia.

Visual Aid: Show slides, large map, or colorful posters and pictures of Indonesia.

Songs: "Wordless Book" song, and learn "Jesus Loves Me" in Indonesian (in the book).

Activity: Make Wordless book: pre-cut pages from colored construction paper and gold gift-wrap paper. Help the children paste the pages together.

Prayer: for Muslim people groups in Indonesia.

Lesson 26: Muslim People Groups--Indonesia.

Story: Lessons 3 and 4 from World Focus book, Muslim People Groups—Indonesia.

Visual Aid: Show slides, large map, or colorful posters and pictures of Indonesia.

Songs: "Jesus Loves Me," and learn "Hari Ini" ("This Is The Day"), both in Indonesian (see Songs).

Activity: Make map page or one of the other activity pages in the book.

Prayer: for Muslim children in Indonesia.

Lesson 27: Malaysia.

Story: "Sold Twice." Flashcard story of Malaysia. Order from OMF (see Visual Aids—Flashcards section.)

Visual Aid: Flashcard book "Sold Twice."

Songs: "Bring Them In" and "Hari Ini" (see Songs section).

Activity: Play a people group game for "Fruit-Basket Upset," using names of people groups.

Prayer: for the hidden peoples in Malaysia.

Lesson 28: Unreached Peoples of North Korea.

Story: "Young Ki's Courage." Flashcard story of Korea (see Visual Aids—Flashcards section).

Visual Aid: Flashcard book "Sold Twice/Young Ki's Courage."

Songs: "Bring Them In" and "Little Missionaries."

Activity: Bring cooked rice and chop sticks for each child to practice eating with them.

Prayer: for the unreached peoples in North Korea.

Lesson 29: Muslims.

Story: "Mustapha's Secret," Lesson 1. Flashcard story of a Muslim boy in North Africa. Order from William Carey Library or Gospel Missionary Union.

Visual Aid: Use the pictures in the flashcard story book.

Songs: Learn "Jesus Loves Children" (*Salvation Song Book* #3, p. 56), and review foreign songs.

Activity: Make "Hello" booklet using the word "hello" in various languages (see instructions in Sampler section).

Prayer: for Muslims in Morocco.

Lesson 30: Muslims.

Story: "Mustapha's Secret," Lesson 2.

Visual Aid: Flashcard book.

Songs: "Jesus Loves Children" and "Far Away."

Activity: Make prayer wheels, using small pictures of people groups (use instructions in Sampler section).

Prayer: for Muslims everywhere.

Lesson 31: Muslims.

Story: "Mustapha's Secret," Lesson 3.

Visual Aid: Flashcard book.

Activity: Make model bush village, using a large stiff cardboard (such as a flattened corregated box), bathroom tissue tubes and cone-shaped paper drinking cups for huts. Use sand for the ground, and twigs and green paper for trees and leaves. Use green sponge pieces for bushes, and stones for boulders. Make animals and people from pipe stem cleaners.

Songs: Learn Portuguese song "Deus e' Tao Bom," to the tune of "God is So Good" (see Songs section), and "Far Away."

Prayer: for Muslim children in Morrocco.

Lesson 32: Muslims.

Story: "Mustapha's Secret," Lessons 4 and 5.

Visual Aid: Flashcard book.

Songs: "Deus e' Tao Bom" and "All the Children Ought to Know"

Activity: Contact Friends of Turkey organization to participate in their pen-pal or letter-sending project.

Prayer: for Muslim peoples in Africa.

Lesson 33: Story of Hudson Taylor.

Story: "Hudson Taylor," Part I (see Visual Aids—Flashcards section).

Visual Aid: Flashcard book.

Songs: Learn "Lai Shin Yesu" (see Songs section), and "Little Missionaries."

Activity:

Prayer: for the hidden peoples in China.

Lesson 34: Story of Hudson Taylor.

Story: "Hudson Taylor," Part II.

Visual Aid: Flashcard book.

Songs: "Lai Shin Yesu" and "Children of A 1,000 Tongues" (see Lesson 2, and change 1,000 to 3,000).

Activity: Read one or two more stories from *From Arapesh to Zuni*, and draw a picture if time.

Prayer: for all the children in China.

Lesson 35: Story of HudsonTaylor.

Story: "Hudson Taylor," Part III.

Visual Aid: Flashcard book.

Songs: Learn "To the East, to the West" (*Salvation Song Book #3*, p. 55). Illustrate song, making large circles like compass. Also: "Lai Shin Yesu."

Activity: Play a game with the People Group flashcards (see Coloring pages).

Prayer: for more missionaries to go to China.

Lesson 36: Story of Hudson Taylor.

Story: "Hudson Taylor," Part IV

Visual Aid: Flashcard book.

Songs: "To the East, to the West" and "Little Missionaries."

Activity: Draw picture of something from story, or eat cooked rice with chop sticks.

Prayer: for the secret "house churches" in China.

Lesson 37: Story of Hudson Taylor.

Story: "Hudson Taylor," Part IV.

Visual Aid: Flashcard book.

Songs: "To the East, to the West" and "Little Missionaries."

Activity: Make up skit of something from the story, and have children act out.

Prayer: for more Bibles to be carried and/or sent to China.

Lesson 38: Story of Hudson Taylor.

Story: "Hudson Taylor," Part V.

Visual Aid: Flashcard book.

Songs: "To the East, to the West" and "Far Away."

Activity: Read one or two more pages from *From Arapesh to Zuni*.

Prayer: for the hidden peoples in China.

Lesson 39: The Poor.

Story: "A Tour of My House," lesson on p. 22 of book *Making Missions Meaningful* (see Books section) and related activities.

Visual Aid: Make two large cardboard-box houses (such as boxes from large appliances), one for house of plenty, and one for house of want. Put some good children's furniture, play dishes, a nice doll, etc., in house of plenty. In house of want, put one dirty dish, one dirty old pot, a jar of dirty water, an old naked doll, and a dirty rag.

Activity: Eat two tablespoons of rice. Draw pictures of foods and water uses that you have in your house.

Songs: "He's Got the Whole World" and "Bring Them In."

Prayer: for the world's hungry people.

Lesson 40: Hindus in India—from World Focus/India.

Story: Parts from Lessons 1 and 2 from the *World Focus* book, *Hindu People Groups—India*.

Visual Aid: Make enlarged map from one of the maps in the book and use slides from India (or posters), as suggested.

Songs: Learn the Hindi song for "Jesus Loves Me" as suggested, and review "Little Missionaries."

Activity: Make the boarding passes as suggested, and reproduce one of the India maps in the book and do the suggested activity.

Prayer: for missionaries to go to all the people groups in India.

Lesson 41: Hindus in India—from World Focus/India.

Story: Use parts of Lessons 3 or 4 in the World Focus Book, Hindu People Groups—India.

Visual Aid: Have a paper bag Hindu puppet ready or use other Hindu figure, and posters or pictures from India.

Songs: Learn "Yumi Kristen" and Hindi "Jesus Loves Me."

Activity: Each child make the Hindu paper bag puppet, and one other activity page from the book, as time allows.

Prayer: for all Hindus in India.

Lesson 42: Hindus in India—from *The Gospel Ship.*

Story: Use parts of Lessons #1 and 13 on India from the puppet story from *The Gospel Ship.*

Visual Aid: Use puppets and the Gospel Ship stage prop.

Songs: "Yumi Kristen" and Hindi "Jesus Loves Me" (see Songs section).

Activity: Choose activity page from *Hindu People Groups/India* book.

Prayer: for all the children in India.

Lesson 43: Hindus in India—from *The Gospel Ship.*

Story: Use parts of Lessons #14 or 16, India puppet story from *The Gospel Ship.*

Visual Aid: Use puppets and the Gospel Ship.

Songs: "Far Away" and "Yumi Kristen."

Activity: Choose activity from *Hindu People Groups/India* book.

Prayer: for missionaries to go to Hindus in India.

Lesson 44: Chinese Peoples.

Story: *Escape By Night*, Part I, Crossroads Publishers (see Curricula and Publishers). Put up map in advance of lesson. Go through preparation, story, and application.

Visual Aid: Use posters with the curriculum.

Songs: "Hidden Peoples" song and "Lai Shin Yesu."

Activity: Make Chinese hat (directions in *Escape By Night*) and do one activity page from book. Save all pages to make book later on.

Prayer: Have children color two provinces on China map and pray for people in those provinces.

Lesson 45: Chinese Peoples.

Story: *Escape By Night*, Part II.

Visual Aid: Use posters with the curriculum.

Songs: "Children Of A 1000 (3,000) Tongues," and "Lai Shin Yesu."

Activity: Make sampan out of 1/2-gallon milk cartons (instructions in *Escape By Night*). Do one activity page from book.

Prayer: Color two more provinces on China map and pray for Chinese refugees.

Lesson 46: Chinese Peoples.

Story: *Escape By Night*, Part III.

Visual Aid: Use posters with the curriculum.

Songs: "Lai Shin Yesu" and "To the East, to the West."

Activity: Make lanterns as described in *Escape By Night* and do one activity page.

Prayer: Color and pray for two more China provinces.

Lesson 47: Chinese Peoples.

Story: *Escape By Night*, Part IV (light an incense stick before story).

Visual Aid: Use posters in the curriculum.

Songs: "Lai Shin Yesu," stanza 2 and "Children of 3000 Tongues."

Activity: Color large paper dragon (in kit). Have all children sit on floor around it or hang it up on wall. If time, do one activity page.

Prayer: Color and pray for two more China province and for the Chinese who escape from China.

Lesson 48: Chinese Peoples.

Story: *Escape By Night*, Part V.

Visual Aid: Use posters with the curriculum.

Songs: "To The East, To The West" and "Lai Shin Yesu."

Activity: Write and color Chinese characters as suggested in book. Do an activity sheet.

Prayer: Color and pray for people in two more China provinces.

Lesson 49: Chinese Peoples.

Story: *Escape By Night*, Part VI. Burn incense stick during story.

Visual Aid: Use posters with the curriculum.

Songs: "Deus e' Tao Bom" and "To The East, To The West."

Activity: Make book cover from directions in *Escape By Night* (make it simpler, if possible). Do another worksheet.

Prayer: Color and pray for people in one or two more Chinese provinces.

Lesson 50: Chinese Peoples.

Story: *Escape By Night*, Part VII. Burn incense stick during story.

Visual Aid: Use posters with the curriculum.

Songs: "Deus e' tao Bom" and "Lai Shin Yesu."

Activity: Explain "God's Messenger" sheet from the *Escape By Night* book and draw pictures. Then complete all unfinished activity pages and tie book together using yarn laced through 2 punched holes.

Prayer: Complete coloring any unfinished China provinces on the map and pray for them.

Lesson 51: Hindus in Calcutta, India (Easter Lesson).

Story: Lesson # 17 on Calcutta, India from *The Gospel Ship*.

Visual Aid: Use puppets and the Gospel Ship stage prop.

Songs: Sing Hindi "Jesus Loves Me," and "Jesus Loves the Unreached Children" (see Songs section).

Activity: Choose activity page from *Hindu People Groups/India* book.

Prayer: Pray for all the children in Calcutta, India.

Lesson 52: People Group Lesson from *You Can Change the World.*

Story: Any people group lesson from *You Can Change the World* (Idea: start a new year of lessons by going through the book).

Visual Aid: Reproduce the page from the book on overhead transparencies, or secure appropriate slides.

Songs: "Blessed to Be a Blessing" and "Jesus Loves the Unreached Children" (see Songs).

Activity: If using the book for another whole year, get the companion coloring books.

Prayer: Use the prayer requests mentioned in the book.

13

LESSONS

INTRODUCTION TO MISSIONS FOR PRE-SCHOOL AND KINDERGARTEN

INVOLVE CHILDREN

All children learn best by being involved, and this is especially true when teaching pre-school, kindergarten and primary grades. Although it may not seem that way, teachers' influence on these little children is very significant, so they must be role models. Children learn first at home from their parents, then from their teachers, in whatever setting that may be. You need good and thorough planning, goals, and plenty of helpers. Then find the resources, and that's what this book is all about. I must assume that my readers are already good, adequately trained teachers—then I just give them the resources and suggestions on how to use them. Use only one or parts of two for the introductory lesson.

SUGGESTIONS FOR HIDDEN PEOPLES INTRODUCTORY LESSONS FOR PRE-SCHOOLERS

1. Show the video, "God's Kaleidoscope," after introductory remarks (see VIDEOS).
   - use the country/people group talked about in the video as a review quizz.
   - make a poster with a spinner, paste on a picture of each major block of people groups, and play games with this (see illustration).
   - teach the theme song, "God's Kaleidoscope," playing the music of the video to sing along.
   - sing "Jesus Loves Me," repeating the chorus by singing "Yes, Jesus loves them." Stress how Jesus loves not only "me" but "them."
   - may do role-playing of people from different people groups.
   - may reproduce "Hidden Peoples" page of children for coloring papers.
2. Use the "Hidden Peoples" lesson (see following pages for grades 1 - 6).
   - simplify and shorten it for pre-schoolers.
   - use paper bag puppets or any puppets available to illustrate different people groups (see VISUAL AIDS/Puppets for where to get international faces from CEF Press for paperbag puppets).
   - sing "Jesus Loves the Little Children," using the four colored construction papers for the colors mentioned in the song. Let four children stand up to hold these.
   - let some children hold some of the puppets also, while singing the song.
   - may also use the Spinner Poster to play a game.
   - may omit the "Handful of Rice" part of the lesson.
   - use the parts of the lesson which are easy for pre-schooler to understand.
   - make and use the teaching posters illustrating the five major blocks of "Hidden Peoples."

- may also use the "Hidden Peoples" coloring page, to color or as a take-home paper.
3. Use *What Language Does God Speak?* as an introductory lesson (PUBLISHERS/William Carey Library).
  - if desired, order the rental slide show which accompanies the the story.
  - use puppets or posters of different people groups.
  - if possible, get a Bible or New Testament in another language, also bring your English Bible, to illustrate the story.
  - sing "Yes, Jesus Loves Me," then sing "Yes, Jesus Loves Them" the second time.
  - then teach "Jesus Loves Me" in another language (words for Spanish and Japanese in Songs/Music section).
  - do role-playing of the story, sending a "missionary" to a "Hidden People" group.
  - reproduce one page of the story book as a coloring or take-home paper.
4. Use *From Arapesh to Zuni* and select several stories as you have time for, including the other activities in the typical format (to order, see PUBLISHERS/William Carey Library).
  - use the rest of the stories as future follow-up "Hidden Peoples" lessons.
  - use posters, puppets, songs and activities suggested above.
  - may use the Spinner Poster to play people group games.
  - review past lessons/people groups in the future lessons—what language, name of group, country, etc. Children can easily memorize this information if reviewed often.

Remember, due to the short attention span of a pre-schooler, make no part of the lesson more than <u>five</u> minutes long.

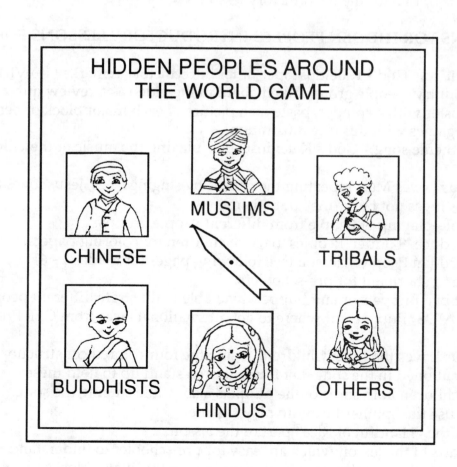

A typical format might be
- singing 2–5 minutes
- story 5–8 minutes
- singing (stand up and/or act out song) 5 minutes
- role play the story (or other appropriate action) 5 minutes
- prayer (children pray also) 2–5 minutes
- activity (handwork or game or ethnic snack) 5 minutes

Have a theme, a goal, thorough preparation, good visual aids and a follow-up activity. Frequently ask for feedback to see how well they are understanding the lesson, as well as the concept of people groups.

SAMPLE INTRODUCTORY MISSIONS LESSON FOR PRE-SCHOOLERS AND FIRST GRADES

INVOLVE CHILDREN

All children learn best by being involved, and this is especially true when teaching pre-school, kindergarten and first grades. Although it may not seem that way, teachers' influence on these little children is very significant, so they must be role models. Children learn first at home from their parents, then from their teachers, in whatever setting that may be. You need good and thorough planning, goals, and plenty of helpers. Then find the resources, and that's what this book is all about. I must assume that my readers are already good, adequately trained teachers—then I just give them the resources and suggestions how to use them. Use only one or parts of two for the introductory lesson.

Suggestions For Hidden Peoples Introductory Lessons (use only one of these for each lesson and keep it brief)

1. Show the video "God's Kaleidoscope," after introductory remarks (see VIDEOS for how to get it).
    - use the country/people group talked about in the video as a review quiz.
    - make a poster with a spinner, and a picture of each country/people group mentioned in the video (optional—see illustration).
    - teach the theme song "God's Kaleidoscope," playing the first part (music) of the video to sing along.
    - sing the the song "Jesus Loves Me," repeating the chorus by singing "Yes, Jesus loves them." Stress how Jesus loves not only "me" but also "them."
    - may do role-playing of people from different people groups.
    - may reproduce "Hidden Peoples" page of children for coloring papers.

2. Use the "Hidden Peoples" lesson (see following pages for grades 1–6)
    - simplify and shorten it for pre-schoolers.
    - use paper bag puppets or any puppets available to illustrate different people groups (see VISUAL AIDS/Puppets for where to get International faces from CEF Press for paperbag puppets).
    - sing "Jesus Loves the Little Children," using the four colored construction papers for the colors mentioned in the song. Let four children stand up to hold these.
    - let some children hold some of the puppets also, while singing the song.
    - may omit the "Handful of Rice" part of the lesson.
    - use the parts of the lesson which are easy for pre-schooler to understand.
    - make and use the teaching posters illustrating the five major blocks of "Hidden Peoples."
    - may also use the "Hidden Peoples" coloring page, to color or as a take-home paper.

3. Use *What Language Does God Speak?* as an introductory lesson (PUBLISHERS/William Carey Library).
    - if desired, order the rental slide show which accompanies the the story.
    - use puppets or posters of different people groups.
    - if possible, get a Bible or New Testament in another language, and also bring your English Bible, to illustrate the story.
    - sing "Yes, Jesus Loves Me," then sing "Yes, Jesus Loves Them" the second time.
    - then teach "Jesus Loves Me" in another language (words are in Songs/Music section).

- do role-playing of the story, sending a "missionary" to a "Hidden People" group.
- reproduce one page of the story book as a coloring or take-home paper.

4. Use *From Arapesh to Zuni* and select several stories as you have time, including any other activities mentioned (to order, see PUBLISHERS/William Carey Library).
   - use the rest of the stories as future follow-up "Hidden Peoples" lessons.
   - use posters, puppets, songs and activities suggested above.
   - review past lessons/people groups in the future lessons: what language, name of group, country, etc. Children can easily memorize this information if reviewed often.

5. Other good lessons to teach effectively to pre-schoolers are missions puppet stories. A good book of these is *The Gospel Ship*, which contains 24 scripts, available from Acorn Children's Publications. For a stage/prop, see illustration below.
   Remember, due to the short attention span of a pre-schooler, no part of the lesson should be more than <u>five</u> minutes long.
   A typical format might be:
   - singing 2–5 minutes
   - story 5–8 minutes
   - singing (stand up and/or act out song) 2–4 minutes
   - role play the story 5 minutes

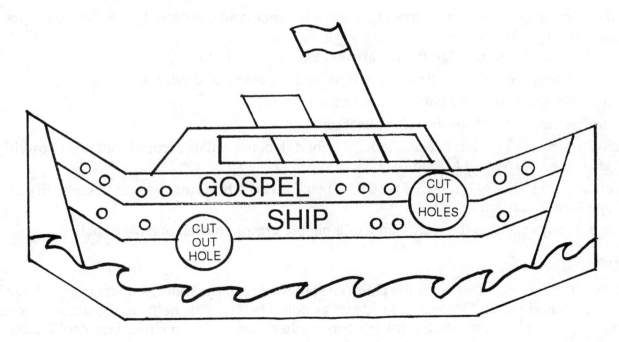

HOW TO MAKE THE "GOSPEL SHIP" PUPPET STAGE PROP:
Out of a large box (from a washer or dryer) cut off one side and the top flaps, leaving 3 sides and bottom flaps as shown, the flaps being the footing for standing. Cut the ship and port holes as shown and cover entire ship with white shelf paper, coloring in the design with marker pens. The 2 open port holes are for puppets to occasionally appear, as the script suggests. Attach a dowel for a flag pole, and design an appropriate flag. When opened as shown, the bottom flaps will support it for standing on a table. Make copies of your script and tape to the back of the "ship" for reading during presentation. May substitute stuffed animals for puppets. Use different tones of voices for each puppet. The captain should wear a white uniform and captain's cap.

- prayer (children pray also) 2 - 4 minutes
- activity (handwork or game or ethnic snack) 5 minutes

Have a theme, a goal, thorough preparation, good visual aids and a follow-up activity. Frequently ask questions to see how well they are understanding the lesson, as well as the concept of People Groups.

INTRODUCTORY LESSON ON HIDDEN PEOPLES FOR GRADES 1 THROUGH 6

The following lesson is designed to introduce the concept of unreached people groups (called Hidden Peoples in this lesson). It includes the formation of a "Hidden Peoples Club." (The author has used this as an introductory lesson when she has been invited to speak in churches she does not normally attend. Many teachers have said that after this initial lesson they have continued to use the "Hidden Peoples Club" idea as a missions emphasis point in their weekly lessons.)

Materials to have on hand

—hand puppets of foreign children (heads to make international paper bag puppets are found in the book *World's Children*, from CEF Press);

—Bible;

— five large posters with pictures of children of other lands, especially the five major people groups mentioned;

—world globe (with Hidden People areas covered with cloth);

—colored sheets of construction paper (red, yellow, black, and white);

—jar of rice (or individual baggies of rice);

—another empty bowl for the rice collection;

—empty jar with Hidden Peoples label attached (labels available from Frontier Fellowship/ U.S. Center for World Mission);

—self-stick "HIDDEN PEOPLES CLUB" labels for each child (make them from "HELLO"-type labels—optional);

—slips of paper with a different name of a people group on each one (optional).

Preparation

Before the program, hide one of the children somewhere in the room, and arrange to have her/ him pop up and shout, "Help, I'm hidden!" as noted below. This helps to illustrate the concept "hidden" to children and they think it's fun. Rather than hiding a child, you could use one of the paper bag puppets, and hide it behind you.

Program

Hi! I'm (name), and you are lucky today because each of you gets to join a club! You all like clubs, don't you? I'll tell you the name of the club later and you will each get a club label before you leave!

Today, we're going to find out who "Hidden Peoples" are. (Beginning here, hidden child or puppet quickly pops up and down at each mention of the word "hidden" and shouts "Help, I'm hidden!" Leader should have her back to the hidden child and pretend not to see her pop up.)

Wait, did I hear someone shout something? Well, anyway, did you know that there are many boys and girls in the world who never heard about Jesus? We call them "Hidden Peoples." (Child pops up.)

Did you hear someone again? I didn't see anyone.

"Hidden Peoples" ("Help, I'm hidden!")

Who is that? Is that a Hidden Person? Would you like to have the Hidden Person come out? You know, Hidden People do not have a Sunday school or Bible or church like we do....If you would like to have that Hidden Person come out, you will have to tell her about Jesus and say some "magic" words. The magic words are "Jesus Loves you."

All shout the magic words together and child comes out from hiding.

Now we'll play another game to find out who the "Hidden Peoples" are.

Divide the group in approximate fifths and have two-fifths close their eyes. Briefly hold up a Bible, then put it away. Then have all open their eyes and ask if the people with their eyes closed knew what you had held in your hand. *This is the way about half of the world is, because they have never seen a Bible, so we call them "Hidden Peoples."* (Have them repeat "Hidden Peoples" after you each time you say it.)

Now have the same group close their ears with their fingers. Whisper something to someone near you. Then, after they open their ears, ask if they heard you. *"Hidden Peoples" are like this, too, as they cannot hear about Jesus, since no one has gone to them to tell them in a way that they can understand.* (Have them say together again: "Hidden Peoples.")

Say a phrase in another language (or have someone who speaks another language say a phrase in that language) and ask if the children understood. *People who cannot understand about the Bible and Jesus because they speak another language are also called "Hidden Peoples."* You might add that the Bible is yet to be translated into about 1000 languages. (Make sure children understand what you mean by "Bible translation.")

Show large posters of foreign children, identifying the 5 major blocs of people groups and talk about each. (See posters illustration, using pictures from magazines.) By this time, ask the children to respond with "Hidden Peoples" each time you talk about a "Hidden Peoples" group. Show world globe with each of the "Hidden Peoples" areas covered by a different colored cloth. As you talk about the following groups, some of the older children may be able to find the appropriate places on the globe. If there is time, review briefly who each group worships (such as Muslims praying five times a day, and to whom do they pray).

MUSLIMS *live in north Africa and throughout Asia. There are 3,800 Unreached People Groups remaining among the MUSLIMS.*

TRIBAL *peoples live in many of the southeast Asian islands and elsewhere all over the world. There are almost 2,700 Unreached TRIBAL People Groups remaining.*

Most **HINDUS** *live in India. There are about 1,800 Unreached HINDU People Groups remaining.*

There are about 900 Unreached **CHINESE** *People Groups. And where do most CHINESE live? In China, of course!*

BUDDHISTS *live in southeast Asia, part of central China, Mongolia, Korea, and Japan. Experts figure there are about 900 Unreached BUDDHIST People Groups remaining.*

That leaves about 900 **Other Unreached People Groups** *scattered all over - for a total of 11,000 Unreached People Groups.*

You may refer to these as being "hidden" ("hidden" from the Gospel).

Have all stand up and sing "Jesus Loves the Little Children" while a few children stand in front holding red, brown, yellow, black and white colored paper and/or international puppets. Ask them which puppets and/or which children on the posters they can identify by the colors they are singing about in the song. Also, which peoples groups are they from? Sing the song, including the color "brown."

Now ask the question: *"If there are so many "Hidden People" Groups, what can we do to reach them for Jesus?"*

"Here is what some Christians in Burma (Myanmar) did." Tell "The Plot" story ("The Burma Plan"—see page 23) in a way the children can understand.

Do role-playing and give small baggies of rice (loose rice will spill on the floor) to a few children, and have them pretend to be the Burmese people bringing rice to their church so others may hear about Jesus. Have children come to the front to put their rice into an empty bowl or basket you have with you.

"Here in America we don't eat much rice, so what could we do to collect something to get the Gospel to the 'Hidden Peoples'?" Ask discussion questions about this as to what everyone could do.

Illustrate how we give loose change instead of rice. First ask what we can save instead of rice. Offer an empty jar to the department (or group), and discuss children saving their extra change for the "Hidden Peoples." Tell them they will get their own "Hidden Peoples" jar labels to take home only after they bring their change the first time. Ask them to involve their entire family with loose change collection in a jar.

We have one more thing to do, and it is the most MOST IMPORTANT part if you are to be a mem-

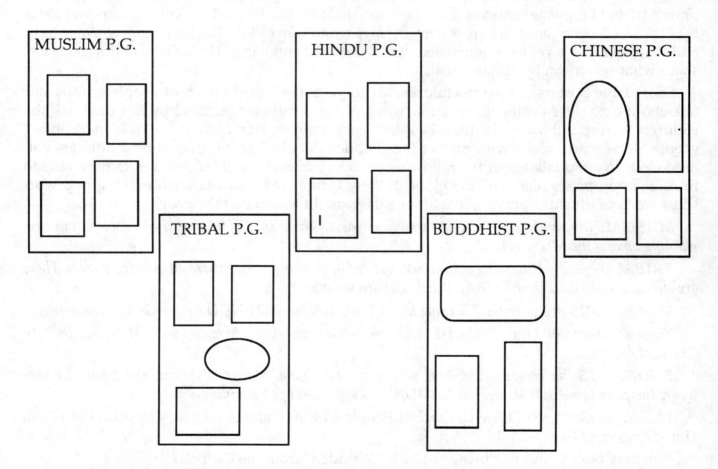

Make the posters out of colorful heavy tagboard, at least 14"x21", making large lettering, and pasting pictures such as from "National Geographic" magazines.

ber of the 'Hidden Peoples' Club. That is, we're going to PRAY for the 'Hidden Peoples.'

Suggest a possible sentence to say, such as "Dear God, please help the 'Hidden Peoples' to hear about Jesus, and send missionaries to them." Ask them to have their families join them at home to pray daily for the "Hidden Peoples." As a follow-up, on future Sundays or once a month you might give children names of new people groups to pray for. Have the names printed on slips of paper. Get names from the *Global Prayer Digest* (available from Frontier Fellowship/U.S. Center for World Mission). Assist the children with pronunciations.

Now that you are all members of the 'Hidden Peoples' Club, you will get your official labels.

Put stick-on labels on children as they leave, or use pin-on labels.

You will want to teach missions and have missionary projects regularly. Many suggestions are in the article "Give Kids a Heart for Missions" in Supplemental Readings section. Make sure the emphasis is on the "Hidden Peoples" (unreached peoples).

ADDITIONAL SUGGESTIONS FOR TEACHING MISSIONS (UNREACHED PEOPLES) TO GRADES K–6

A special "Hidden Peoples" Sunday. Ideas:

—Have children come in costumes. (Make costumes in class over a period of several Sundays).

—Practice and put on a play with or without costumes.

—Use puppets for plays.

—Special filmstrip or movie.

Prepare self-adhesive labels for each child designating them members of the "Hidden Peoples" Club, or use pin-on labels.

Introduce loose change jar and have available every Sunday.

Give the "Hidden Peoples" jar labels to each child only the first time they bring loose change. Emphasize they are to use jar with their families at home.

Have each department or class (or church, if small) "adopt" a special Hidden Peoples group to pray for.

—Send for information about the "Adopt-A-People" program from the U.S. Center for World Mission (see "Adopt-A-People" pages).

—Send for pictures, slides and videos about the people group you decide to adopt.

—Correspond with missionaries or missionary agencies focusing on that group.

—Have families and departments send money from loose change jars to the special Hidden Peoples fund selected, or to the Frontier Fellowship Hidden Peoples Project (Frontier Fellowship, 1605 Elizabeth, Pasadena, CA 91104).

Do "tape-sponding" with a selected missionary. (Children love to put their voices on tapes to missionaries.)

—Use one tape to send back and forth.

—Encourage missionary to list prayer requests.

—Have children pray for those requests.

Ask missionaries to send simple songs in foreign language which children can learn.

If plan is used in Children's or Junior Church, an on-going missionary adventure story can be used, telling one 5- or 10-minute episode each Sunday. Any curriculum in this book could be used. Use the mystery of anticipating another episode, or a contest for attendance.

Use occasional videos.

Tell a story from a missionary story book. (Illustrate if possible.)

Have occasional puppet plays or missions skits.

Always have on hand a world globe or large world map. Help children find countries or areas being discussed and pray over them. Play games with the globe.

Make your own posters with pictures from old *National Geographic* magazines, etc.

—Make one large poster for each of the five major people group blocs—tribal, Muslim, Hindu, Chinese and Buddhist.

—Use colorful tag-board to mount them. Try especially to use pictures involving children, or interesting to children.

Always try to make use of missionary speakers in your area. The week before or after the missionary visits, use a story from the same country from which the speaker comes.

Correlate activities, songs, crafts, pictures, and/or snacks with the particular country or culture discussed. Build miniatures of houses or transportation, also related.

Create a global awareness center for special missions activities, such as audio visuals.

Involve the children as often as possible. Let them hold things. Involve them in skits, puppet plays, role-playing, costume plays, etc.

Repeatedly ask for feedback from the children, to ascertain if they understand the concept of "Hidden Peoples."

The following additional suggestions were submitted by Shari Schorr, Children's Missionary Fellowship at Antioch Alliance Church in Logan, Ohio:

-Involve the 7th to 12th graders in church to be aides in the children's program, asking that they committ themselves to a certain time allottment (eg. 1 month), that they teach some of the lessons, and that they help with all programs and projects throughout the year.

-"Match His Weight": have the children raise funds for a missions project which match the weight of someone on the church staff (the pastor!).

-Prepare for and perform special missions music in a special missions worship time in church.

-Carry in a parade of international flags for the above, which the children have made. Have children dress in international costumes for this.

-Do a "Share-A-Spare for Missions," for the Halloween Party in October.

-Have an open house after about a year of regular missions lessons, setting up displays of each country and/or people group studied so far. Serve cookies and punch.

-Adopt an M.K. of one of the missionary families of your church and make a friendship sheet to send to him/her. Have each child either draw a small picture or write a short note on it. Let him know your group is regularly praying for him.

-Use your denomination's missionary handbook or praying guide.

-Correspond with other missionaries from your denomination.

-Use flashcard stories and Kids World Missionary paper from CAM.

-Learn and present "Kids' Praise 6" missions musical (perhaps at a missions conference).

-Play international games with the adults in the afternoon of your missions conference day.

-Have a junior missions retreat or a 24-hour missions campout. Have 7th–12th graders assist with this and the games.

-Plan to get the children to be missionaries in their own community. Do some of the following things:

- food drive for your missionary home on furlough, or for your local county food pantry.

- repair and paint old bikes, then donate them to needy organizations, or sell them to raise missions funds. Have 7th–12th graders assist with this.

-Have teachers and aides teach on a 3-month rotation.

-Set goals with plans and ideas to achieve the goals.

SAMPLE HIDDEN PEOPLES LESSON FOR JUNIOR HIGHERS

Materials to have on hand: paper plates, picture posters of foreign peoples, world globe with megaspheres of unreached peoples covered, empty jar and jar labels, and some *Global Prayer Digests* (available from Frontier Fellowship/U.S. Center for World Mission).

Optional: Preceeding the following lesson, have adults begin by presenting a skit or puppet play of "Tower of Babel."

Purpose of the Bible:

Why did God give us the Bible?

What was His purpose? (study the following Bible passages)

John 3:16

Gen. 12:1-3

Mark 16:15

Dialog

The following script may be used by one or two people (two people designated "A" and "B").

A. *Welcome to Hidden Peoples Day! I'm glad to see all of you here, because we'll let you in on who the "Hidden Peoples" are. In the world today there are approximately 12,000 Hidden People Groups—not 11,000 hidden people, but 11,000 Hidden Peoples or Hidden People Groups. They are called "Hidden Peoples" or "Hidden People Groups" because almost no missionaries ever go to work among them. They have no churches, no Bible, and virtually no chance to hear the Gospel in a way they can understand.*

B. *Now I need the assistance of all of you to help illustrate the picture of the world's unreached or "hidden" peoples.* (Note: Further details for this illustration are on pg. 152.)

—Divide group into fifths and have two out of five close their eyes. Briefly hold up a Bible. Then put the Bible away and have them open their eyes. About 2/5 of the world is made up of Hidden Peoples because they have not seen a Bible in their language or are unable to read.

—Now have the same 2/5 put their fingers in their ears, and you whisper something to another person. Now with ears open, illustrate that about 2/5 of the world cannot "hear" the Word of God for several reasons, including unwritten language and no missionaries.

—Have all stand, then 2/5 **sit down**. *These are* Culturally Distant *Non-Christians, or Unreached* Peoples. *Unreached Peoples are culturally distant because almost no one from their culture is a Christian, or almost no one who speaks their language is a Christian. Christians who want to share the good news with these non-Christians will have to make a great effort to cross the cultural or language gap.*

*The people who are now **sitting** we call Unreached Peoples. The people who are **standing** we call* Reached *peoples. But just because they are "Reached" doesnt mean they are all Christians. It simply means that they are all culturally near to the church; there are a significant number of Christians who speak these peoples' languages and who come from these peoples' cultures. No one has to learn a new language or learn a new culture in order for everyone to have a chance to hear the Gospel. There are Christians in each of these groups to share the Gospel with non-Christians in that group.*

—Have half of those still standing sit down. *Okay. Those who just sat down are Culturally Near Non-Christians. They are from Reached groups, but they themselves are not Christians. In other words, they could be your unsaved neighbors.*

—Finally, since we can never tell for sure who is or who is not a real Christian, the people who are still standing represent "Christians" of all types. Some of these—maybe even many of them—are "Christians" in name only. They haven't necessarily received Jesus as their Lord and Savior. Maybe they'd just say, "I'm a Christian because I'm not a Buddhist!" Others really do know Jesus and are committed to following Him. Of all the people we have here in this room, they are the ones who are going to be able to tell others about Jesus. Cut up paper plate #1 (as in illustration) to give another illustration. Explain that all the statistics you've shared are approximate. Have all sit down.

—Ask for six volunteers from the "unreached" two-fifths to come up to the front to hold paper plates. Explain each of the six blocs of unreached peoples.

Question. Out of the Culturally Near Non-Christians, the "Christians" who are Christians in name only, and the Christians who really know Jesus, who should we send to these Unreached Peoples to evangelize them? (Answer: The Committed.)

Okay. And of the six blocs, where do you think we are sending them? (Correct answer: Everywhere except to the Muslims.)

There are so few missionaries working among the Muslims, every missionary who is working among Muslims has about a million Muslims to evangelize. Show paper plate #2.

It looks pretty hopeless....

A. *Wait! Wait! It isn't!*

B. *How can you say that? What can we do?*

A. *I have an idea that I think will work. Christians in Burma are doing this. They are collecting rice to send missionaries to people who haven't heard the Gospel.* Show small bags of rice he brought along.

B. What does collecting rice have to do with sending missionaries?

A. Rice is worth a lot in Burma. I mean, that's almost all they eat.

B. Yeah. But we don't eat much rice. It's not worth a whole lot around here.

A. So what if we saved pizza? No. Seriously. Do any of you guys have any loose change in your pockets? Any pennies, nickels, dimes...? If every family saved up all their loose change, we'd have quite a bit of money to send missionaries....

B. What are you suggesting? That maybe we could have a jar to save change for the Hidden Peoples?

A. Sure! Why not? Save money for missions purposes! Distribute Hidden Peoples Loose Change jars for kids to take home.

A. The most important thing we can do is pray for the Hidden Peoples. Have volunteers pray.

Note: Besides the above suggestions, you may also use the slide-tape show or video, "That All May Hear" from WEC, or "The Final Frontiers" from The U.S. Center for World Mission.

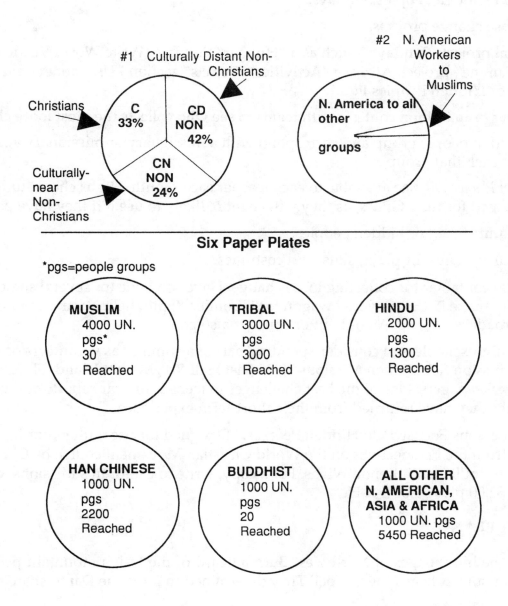

Note: See page 148 for statistical breakdown of world figures. It can be safely stated now that one out of every 3500 True Christians is a missionary; and nine of every 100 missionaries is reaching the unreached, the other 91 are working in reached groups. For a vivid portrayal of these and other figures, send for the 1989 full-color *AD 2000* poster from the U.S. Center for World Mission.

ADDITIONAL SUGGESTIONS FOR TEACHING MISSIONS TO JUNIOR HIGH AND HIGH SCHOOL GROUPS

—Use script for the junior high presentation (page 13).

__Use 8 paper plates according to make the diagram on page 137.

—Adapt the suggestions listed for youth.

__Make flashcards or posters, using "Most That Heaven Can Boast Over" from pages 141.

—Have humorous skits and games to illustrate parts of the world that are unreached.

—Have special Hidden Peoples Sundays.

—Sponsor loose change projects.

—Have special projects Sundays—such as a "Hunger" Sunday. (Write World Vision for "Planned Famine" project. Also see "Activities/Projects" section.) Use money saved from not eating for Hidden Peoples Fund.

—Have hunger or marathon contests with teams to see who collects the most loose change.

—Adopt a hidden people group and correspond with a missionary or missionary agency who is trying to reach that group.

—Make *Global Prayer Digests* available to each teacher each month. High school students should be charged for their GPD's, as they will be more likely to use it if they have paid for it.

—Emphasize unreached or hidden peoples.

—Have special Sundays for plays, skits, and costumes.

—Use a special container for collecting loose change. Have someone (or several someones) from the group make it. (Ex: Covered wagon for "Frontiers"; pith helmet; small radio set for missionary broadcasting, etc. An old butter churn is also good.)

—Encourage high-schoolers to consider spending part of a summer as volunteers or short-termers on a mission field. "Teen Missions" (885 East Hall Rd., Merritt Island, FL 32953-8418) and others take teenagers. One of the best challenges to teens is to hear reports of those who have gone after they have returned from their short-term experience.

—Use "Four Lessons Focused On Hidden Peoples." Designed for use with junior highers, it was adapted from the Perspectives on the World Christian Movement course by Christy Dueck, Ginette Goulet, and Brenda Wiens. For a copy, write to Children's Missions Resource Center. Cost: $2.00 plus $2.00 S & H.

THE BURMA PLAN

Christians in the hill villages of Northwest Burma heard of the Dai, a mountain people to the north who had not yet heard the Gospel. They determined to go to the Dai to share the Gospel with them. They needed prayer and financial support. The Christians live simply and eat only two simple rice meals each day. How can they afford to be missionaries? Here is what they do. As they prepare each meal, they set aside a handful of rice, using this simple act as a reminder to pray for their missionaries. These small handfuls, pooled together and sold by the church once a month, raise support not only for the Dai work, but many other projects to hidden tribes. In North America, we don't eat much rice. But we do have loose change jingling in our pockets and our purses at the end of each day. We can save our loose change in a jar each day to help us remember to pray and to help pay for work among hidden peoples.

14
ACTIVITIES

MOST

THAT

HEAVEN

CAN

BOAST

OVER

MUSLIM
3,800 UPG*

TRIBAL
2,700 UPG*

HINDU
1,800 UPG*

CHINESE
900 UPG*

BUDDHIST
900 UPG*

OTHERS
900 UPG*

GAME SUGGESTIONS FOR
MOST THAT HEAVEN CAN BOAST OVER

MOST — **(Muslims)**
THAT — **(Tribals)**
HEAVEN — **(Hindus)**
CAN — **(Chinese)**
BOAST — **(Buddhist)**
OVER — **(Others)**
* Indicates Unreached People Groups

DIRECTIONS
For games, you may reproduce the preceding two pages on colorful card-stock paper, cutting apart on dotted lines. You may print them back-to-back for some games. such as the following or for teaching the slogan "Most That Heaven Can Boast Over" as a clue to "Muslim, Tribal, Hindu, Chinese, Buddhist, Others." You may also enlarge the pages for poster teaching.

Game #1
Pass the flashcards around a circle. Stop at a given (musical?) signal. Kids holding cards read a megasphere of card s/he has. Play it first with "group" side up, then play it with "code words" side up. Then:

Versions:

1. Name 1 specific people group from it (ex. Muslim—Kurd)

2. Holder of the card prays a sentence prayer for that group.

3. Tell 1 thing that megasphere believes/teaches (ex. reincarnation/Hindu).

4. Name a missionary/agency working with those people (ex. Tribals—CMA).

5. Name a country where that religion is prominent (ex. Hindu—India).

6. Come to world map and point out country where that religion is prominent (this also helps geographical positions).

Game #2
Relay race where a card is flashed to both teams. The first player on each team must then do one of the 6 above things. Then each member of the teams must do the same, but not name one that has already been named. When each team has completed that action, another card is flashed and the play continues as before.

Game #3
Individual (this would work well for homeschool) or 2 players race against the clock doing any or all of above 6 things.

Use your creativeness to play other games.

(Used by permission of Bev Gundersen of Monarch Publishing.)

How to Make a "HELLO" Booklet. (P,I)

Have children make small booklet about 6"x 4-1/2" with one page for each "Hello" word, and the cover made of colored construction paper. Have children print "HELLO" on the cover in large letters, and decorate the cover as they wish. Print the following words someplace where they can copy them. Practice saying each word or group of words as you write them (pronunciation guide in parentheses):

Assalamo aleikum (Ah-sa-lah-mo ah-lay-kum)—Urdu (Pakistan).

Guten tag (Goot-en tahk)—Germany.

Buenos dias (Bway-nohs dee-ahs)—Spanish.

Shalom (Sha-lome)—Hebrew.

Su ausue (Soo-ow-sweh)—Basque (Spain).

Eyeyubowan (Eye-yu-bow-an)—Sinhalese (Ceylon).

Woshde-e—Navajo.

Kumsta? (Koom-stah)—Tagalog (Philippines).

Aloha (Ah-lo-ha)—Hawaiian.

Habari (Ha-bah-ree)—Swahili (Tanzania).

Konnichi wa (Koh-nee-shee wah)—Japanese.

Dziendobry (Jahneh-doh-bree)—Yoruba (Nigeria).

Ciao (Chow)—Italian.

Apa Kabar (Ah-pah Iah-bar)—Malay (Indonesia).

Bonjour (Bohn-zhoor)—French.

He (Hi)—Indonesian.

Namestey(Nahmestay)--Hindi (India).

Oga(Oh-gah)--Yoruba(Nigeria).

LET CHILDREN MAKE THEIR DESIGNS ON COVER OF BOOK

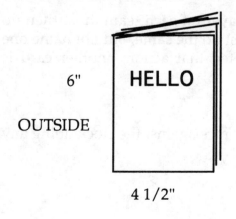

6"

OUTSIDE

HELLO

4 1/2"

GUTENTAG : BUENOS DIAS

GERMAN : SPANISH

INSIDE
ONE PAGE FOR EACH WORD

How to Make a Prayer Wheel

For each child you will need:

—two circles of stiff paper, one white and one colored, each at least 8″ in diameter;

—a brad;

—pictures of individuals from each of the six major blocs of unreached peoples (Muslims, Hindus, Chinese, Buddhists, Tribals, Others). Pictures may be found in old *National Geographic* or mission magazines.

Divide white circles into six areas as shown. Depending on writing ability of children, either provide bloc names, or allow children to write them.

Prepare colored circles with a wedge cut out of top circle (as shown).

Poke holes in the centers of all circles so that, when a brad is inserted, the circles will rotate freely.

Have children glue representative pictures of the various peoples in the appropriate sections of the bottom circle.

Have group members place their top circles on the bottom circles and fasten with a brad.

Use the prayer wheels in class to pray for the Hidden Peoples and then send them home with the children as a reminder for them and their parents to pray.

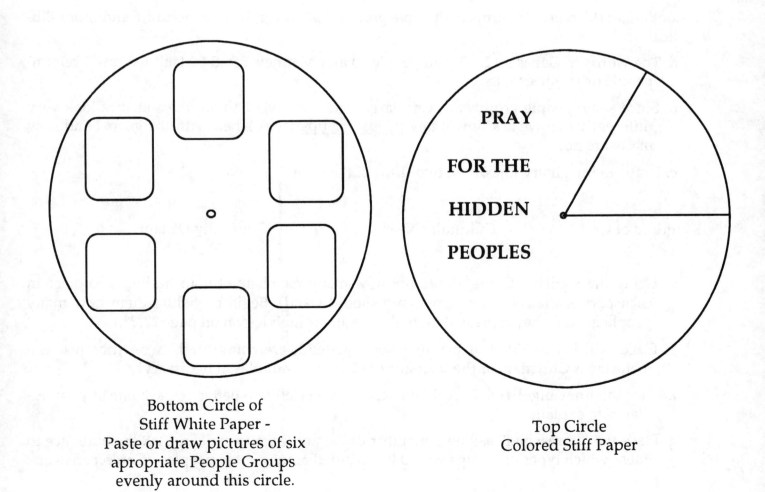

Bottom Circle of
Stiff White Paper -
Paste or draw pictures of six
apropriate People Groups
evenly around this circle.

Top Circle
Colored Stiff Paper

Distribution Exercises (J,S)

1. One way to view the world is to see how many INDIVIDUALS in the world are Christian or non-Christian. The world population today is close to 6 billion people.

   a. Simple illustration: Draw a circle or use a paper plate.

   —Draw lines dividing circle in tenths.

   —1/10 are Bible-believing Christians—those who are active, **committed** disciples, the **potential work force in missions.**

   —2/10 contains **the uncommitted** i.e., the Christians who make a Christian profession, but need to be "renewed or revangelized" in order to help.

   —3/10 includes **the unevangelized**, those who have a minimal knowledge of the gospel, but have not responded to it. These non-Christians are already within the reach of Christian people—the "reached groups."

   —4/10 are **the unreached**, the 2,170 million non-Christians outside the reach of Christians of their own people—these live within "unreached groups"—there is no indigenous, evangelizing church movement within their "nation, people, tribe or tongue." They need the special kind of evangelism called **"missions."**

   —If every Christian were to win his/her neighbor, these **"unreached"** non-Christians would still never have a chance to hear...because of cultural distance.

   —REJOICE! Only FOUR out of ten to go!

2. Looking at the world in terms of "people groups," however, is more accurate and more Biblical.

   a. The words in Genesis 12:1-3 ("all peoples") and Matthew 28:18-20 ("all nations") refer to people or <u>ethnic</u> groups.

   b. Since some people groups are very large, and some very small, the statistics look very different when we ask how many <u>people groups</u> are reached with the gospel and how many are not.

   c. Draw an imaginary line down two-fifths of the room:

Kingdom of God	Culturally Near	Culturally Distant

   d. Using the Statistics Game, figure out how many members of your audience to place in each part of the room (or how many should stand). Begin by telling them how many people groups they represent in total. (See junior high lesson on page ?????.)

   e. Place "Christians" first, explaining that one-tenth are **committed**, two-tenths just call themselves Christian, or **the uncommitted**. (Give examples, if necessary)

   f. Place **the unevangelized**. Explain the term again briefly or, better yet, ask one of your audience to explain.

   g. Place the "unreached" asking a member of the audience to explain. Ask the audience to guess which types of groups would be included among these peoples. (Correct answers:

Muslim, Tribal, Buddhist, Hindu, Han Chinese.) Suggest for each one or two major cultural barriers to the Gospel.

3. "If YOU had 100 CHRISTIAN WORKERS, how would you distribute them among these people groups?" Use circle or other illustration to indicate that only ONE out of 100 Christian workers works among culturally distant non-Christians.

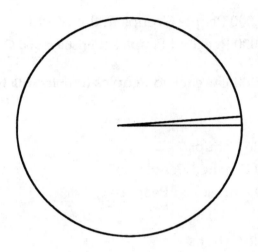

Demographic Statistics Demonstration
(Emphasizing People Groups Rather than Individuals)

This demonstration is especially good for high schoolers and adult groups, though a shortened presentation can also work well with junior highers. Have appropriate proportions of the audience stand up to signify the various statistics you present. (Figure absolute numbers before starting demonstration.)

The World

Total Audience = Total of 24,000 People Groups in the World

54 percent of Audience = 13,000 Reached Peoples (Christians and Culturally-Near Non-Christians)

46 percent of Audience = 11,000 Unreached Peoples (Peoples with No Church that are Culturally Distant from any Church.)

The Buddhist Megasphere

Total Audience = 1,020 People Groups

12 percent of Audience = 120 Reached Peoples

88 percent of Audience = 900 Unreached Peoples

The Han Chinese Megasphere

Total Audience = 3,200 People Groups

72 percent of Audience = 2,100 Reached Peoples

28 percent of Audience = 900 Unreached Peoples

The Hindu Megasphere

Total Audience = 3,300 People Groups

45 percent of Audience = 1,500 Reached Peoples

55 percent of Audience = 1,800 Unreached Peoples

The Muslim Megasphere

Total Audience = 4,030 People Groups

5.7 percent of Audience = 230 Reached Peoples

94.3 percent of Audience = 3,800 Unreached Peoples

The Tribal Megasphere

Total Audience = 6,000 People Groups

55 percent of Audience = 3,300 Reached Peoples

45 percent of Audience = 2,700 Unreached Peoples

Other Western, Asian and African Peoples

Total Audience = 6,450 People Groups

86 percent of Audience = 5,550 Reached Peoples

14 percent of Audience = 900 Unreached Peoples

Missions Awareness Quiz

1. According to the Bible, Christ wants Christians to take the Gospel to:
   a) Their neighbors.
   b) Every country in the world.
   c) Every nation in the world.
   d) Every person in the world.

2. The first reference to missions in the Bible is found in the book of:
   a) Genesis.
   b) Psalms.
   c) Isaiah.
   d) Matthew.

3. Missions is mentioned in that book at least:
   a) Once.
   b) 5 times.
   c) 10 times.
   d) 25 times.

4. "Frontier missions" work is (was):
   a) done among American Indians by Christian settlers as the West was being opened.
   b) mission work among any non-Western people.
   c) needed today by about half the world's population.
   d) what it means to be a missionary and go overseas to tell other people about Jesus.

5. "Hidden" peoples are those groups of people who:
   a) haven't been reached with the Gospel because they live in secluded places.
   b) like to play Hide-and-Seek.
   c) aren't yet Christians because they have never heard of Jesus.
   d) aren't yet Christians and never will be without a cross-cultural witness in their midst.

6. The number of North American missionaries overseas is:
   a) increasing steadily.
   b) in a state of flux.
   c) remaining the same.
   d) decreasing steadily.

7. The most appropriate college major in order to prepare for a career in missions is:
   a) Bible and/or Missions.
   b) Comunity Development.
   c) Art.
   d) Anthropology.

8. I can know I'm called to be involved in missions if:
   a) I'm a Christian.
   b) God speaks to me audibly and tells me to go.
   c) I like travel, "roughing it" and/or learning about other cultures.
   d) I have skills and talents that will enable me to work overseas and to help people.

9. Right now, the most strategic (significant) place for a person to do mission work is in:
   a) Kenya, Africa.
   b) Berlin, West Germany.
   c) Nagaland, India.
   d) Los Angeles, California.

10. The *Global Prayer Digest* is:
    a) an international daily newspaper put out by the U.S. Center for World Mission.
    b) a condensation of some of the best prayers of people who pray for missions.
    c) a booklet with mission stories and daily prayer suggestions for frontier missions.
    d) for adults only.   Adapted from a document by the same name produced by Caleb Project. Used by permission.

MISSIONS AWARENESS QUIZ ANSWERS AND DISCUSSION GUIDE

This program is excellent for high schoolers and adults; adaptable for junior highers.

You will need:

—Questionnaires(Missions Awareness Quiz).

—*Unreached Peoples Poster*(see Visual Aids--Posters).

—*Global Prayer Digest* –at least one sample copy (available from Frontier Fellowship, 1605 Elizabeth St., Pasadena, CA 91104. Subscription: $9/year).

Procedure:

Have everyone fill out a questionnaire.

When they are finished, have someone read Matthew 28:18-20. Now lead a group discussion on their answers to the questions on the questionnaire.

Discussion Guide:

1. Correct answers are (a) and (c). Neighbors reaching neighborswill never achieve the goal of (c). Some people will have to reach across cultural and geographic barriers before every nation can be reached. Talk about the difference between countries(geopolitical entities) and nations (ethnic groups—*ta ethne* in the Greek New Testament). Use the example of India which is one country with more than 3,000 nations in its midst. Before Christians can possibly think of reaching every person (d), they will first have to break into the midst of every nation.

2. Correct answer is (a). People will usually guess all the wrong answers first. The first clear reference to missions (the Gospel for all nations) may be foundin Genesis 12:2-3. (See also Galatians 3:8: "And the scripture...preached the gospel beforehand to Abraham, saying, 'In you shall all the nations be blessed'."

3. Correct answer is (d)! Think of all the passages that talk about contact between the gospel-bearers (Abraham's descendants) and the nations 'round about! Was Joseph a missionary? For another eye-opener, read Psalm 67. Notice all the references to "peoples" and "nations"! We don't realize God's concern for the nations.

4. (c) is most correct, though (a), (b) and (d) are not necessarily incorrect. "Frontier" here refers to the idea that the Gospel is not yet resident ("at home") among the people who are hearing it. There is no church made up of people who are members of thet culture. To put it another way, for a while, anyway, new Christians from that cultureare going to be "pioneers"; they will be establishing new frontiers for their people.

5. Correct answer is (d). "Hidden" here refers to the idea that Christians for some reason just don't seem to "see" these people groups' need for the Gospel. Very few if any missionaries are working among them. (Use the Unreached Peoples poster to show this reality.) Some "hidden" peoples do live in secluded places (a), but that is by no means the only reason a people group might be hidden. Muslims have heard of Jesus (c); in fact, they revere him highly—as a prophet. But they don't trust Him for their salvation.

6. Correct answer is (c). In the past decade, this has primarily been due to the retirement of the "older" force, and the escalation in the number of short-termers. Between 1985 and 1988, the number of career missionaries increased 2,700 while the number of short-termers in-

creased 9,500. These numbers tend to hide the fact that among career missionaries one has to find 80 additional missionaries each year just to stay even.

7. Correct answer is "all of them." There are a great *many* things that would be excellent background for a career in missions. Whatever professional skills one may acquire, however, biblica land cultural training are also necessary.

8. Correct answer is (a) The key phrase is "be involved in missions." *ALL* Christians who are seeking to be obedient to God will be involved in missions. The question is not *whether* to be involved but *how*.

9. Correct answer: "It depends on what you're doing and who you're working with." Nagaland, India (c), is filled with Christians. They have a seminary and Bible school and are sending out missionaries. Who are you trying to reach in Berlin (b)? One people group you might want to target in Berlin is the Turkish Muslims. There are tens of thousands of them there—people who are very difficult to reach in their home country of Turkey but who are easily accessible in Berlin. And Kenya, Africa (a)? Which of the 65 people groups do you have in mind? Some are highly evangelized and have many missionaries working among them; others are almost totally neglected. Los Angeles, California (d), could be more strategic than any of the others. There are more than 140 people groups living there. As with the Turkish Muslims in Berlin, some are far more accessible than they would be if they were back in their "home" territories.

10. Correct answer is (c). Though written mostly for adult readers (d), we know of families who read it in the midst of family devotions. A little "translation" makes most stories easily accessible even to kindergarteners. Pick a page and read an excerpt for your group. Let the group pray for the people group or the item of concern mentioned in that day's reading. (You'll probably want to avoid the missionary biography selections for purposes of this demonstration.) Have order forms and sample copies of the *Digest* available for group members to purchase on the spot. Many Christians have said this is one of the most helpful prayer tools they have ever used.

PRAY FOR THE HIDDEN PEOPLES

15

SUPPLEMENTARY READING

UNITED STATES

Center
for
World
Mission

1605 Elizabeth Street
Pasadena, CA 91104
818/797-1111 • FAX 818/398-2263

1. DEFINITION OF MISSION:

"We need to clarify definition of mission," says Dr. Ralph Winter, " - the Unreached Peoples. We need to educate people (and children) to go where the gospel has never been preached. Missions is going to people groups. Missions is not merely evangelism or missionaries. It is mission agencies and the people they send. Missions is not merely exotic cultures, not merely overseas, or overseas church life or helping choirs overseas. **Missions is not reaching the lost because of how lost they are —it is reaching lost people who do not have any other chance."** Let's not forget to keep this as our true focus.

2. Who do we need to reach?

The "Great Commission" gives us Jesus' direction to make disciples of ALL PEOPLES (or ethnic groups), not countries, as most of us used to think. But because of language and cultural barriers within countries, 11,000 of the 24,000 people groups world wide still have no access to the Gospel.

3. Who are the missionaries?

The real definition: **Men and women who feel called of God to cross some kind of boundaries to tell others of Christ. Takes all kinds of people in all kinds of occupations.**

4. What shall we teach to children?

- Teach them **People Groups** (use "Most That Heaven Can Boast Over," for 6 major blocks)
- Use "Hidden Peoples" lesson
- Use visuals (see the People Group flashcard page—**M T H C B O**)
- Any age can understand about people groups
- Teach "Going, Giving, Praying"
- Teach missions in the home
- Use curricula that focuses on unreached people groups
- Make much use of puppet shows, drama, skits, games and role playing
- Use *Global Prayer Digest*
- Use *Kids For the World* resource book
- Use William Carey Library materials list, and catalog
- Have a missions retreat for kids
- Look through the Country, People Group, and Resource Persons Section

5. Response and participation of children

- What can I do now?
- Can I help missionaries now?
- Can I help "hidden peoples" now?
- Could I be a missionary (now or later)?

6. What is the priority of The Church now?

- Adopting people groups is the practical way for a church, working together with a mission agency, to reach one of the remaining unreached peoples. Resources are available from Mobilization Division at the USCWM.

7. Can children's groups "adopt" people groups?

- see the "Adopt-A-People for Children" article

8. What preparation should teachers of missions have?

- Read books: *In the Gap, From Jerucalem to Irian Jaya, On the Crest of the Wave, Operation World, You Can Change the World,* and the *Perspectives* book.
- take the "Perspectives on the World Christian Movement" course. Send for information to:

U.S. Center for World Mission
1605 Elizabeth Street
Pasadena, CA 91104

HAVE A HEART (for Missions)
OR
TOTAL INVOLVEMENT

Missions education in your Sunday School can be much more than singing a song, taking an offering, listening to a story, or viewing a missionary's slides. Here are seven steps to "missions total involvement:"

1. Get organized.

Establish a missions education committee which would serve as a lisison between the missions committee and the Christian education committee. The committee would be responsible for defining purposes and goals, designing programs and locating resources for helping individuals teach missions at all levels.

2. Train and equip staff.

Have monthly teachers' training meeting for missions or have a regular ten-minute missions session at each regular teachers' meeting. Keep teachers supplied with ideas, bulletins, books, visual aids, current missions projects being done by various groups in the church and other resources.

3. Be creative.

Encourage the use of creative teaching methods like role-playing, panel discussions, field trips, audio-visuals, puppets and drama to educate children about missions.

4. Develop a missions curriculum.

Four major aspects of your missions curriculum should be missions in the Bible, in history, today and within your church family. Design your own plan, integrating curriculum available from publishers, as needed.

5. Relate Sunday school to the church's missions program.

Through a process of year-round education, personal acquaintance, prayer, and financial support, each Sunday school class can be personally involved with the church's missionary family. Each class or department could adopt a missionary family for at least a year. During the church's missions conference, individual classes could be responsible for a display.

6. Design a missions learning resource center.

Develop a room that will merge storage, service and learning. This could even be incorporated into a missions resource/teaching room, housing visual aids, books and artifacts.

7. Involve people personally.

A children's class could specialize in a country, such as Japan, for a quarter. The class could decorate the room with Japanese decor, sing songs in Japanese, eat Japanese food and write to children whose parents are missionaries in Japan. Interest parents to consider taking their children to visit a country they have been studying, for a short- or even long-term basis.

8. Involve as many adult helpers as possible.

This is necessary for all aspects of your Missions program.

9. Adopt an unreached people group.

There are many creative ways to do this, but the best way is to do it in cooperation with the church's missions program. See "Adopt-A-People" page.

10. More missions ideas:

-artifacts—know where they come from and how they are used
-books—missionary biographies and other missionary stories for children
-curios, cassettes from missionaries, table top models and murals
-dolls of different countries
-slides, videos and flags of different countries
-globe of the world for every department
-letters to M.K.'s and their parents.
-maps of the world and individual countries, magazines from missions
-puppets, posters and large pictures from different countries
-enlarged picture of missionary family
-quizzes
-scrapbooks of individual missionaries, international stamps
-illustrated missionary songs and choruses
-take home missionary story papers
-**Bible verses emphasizing missions** on colorful slips of paper: Mark 16:15, Matt. 28:18-20, John 3:16, Acts 1:8, Gen. 12:2, Gen. 12:3, Matt., 24:14, Rev. 7:9, Psalm 67:5, Psalm 67:7, Psalm 105:1, etc.

11. Have a children's missions conference, children's missions fair, or children's missions retreat.

Write to Children's Missions Resource Center for a packet of ideas for a Conference.

12. Take the children on a field trip to a missionary organization.

To make this really meaningful, use it as a special reward for completing certain requirements during a children's missions conference or missions course.

(Parts of the above are adapted from the article "Give a Missions Punch to Your Sunday School Bunch," by Conrad Wilcox, used with permission.)

GIVE THE KIDS A HEART (for Missions)
OR
WHY? WHEN? WHERE? WHAT? HOW?

WHY GIVE KIDS A HEART FOR MISSIONS ?

IT IS IMPORTANT TO VISUALIZE THE FOLLOWING ILLUSTRATION. Although evangelizing our children is vitally important, we must stop NOT there. We MUST BE:

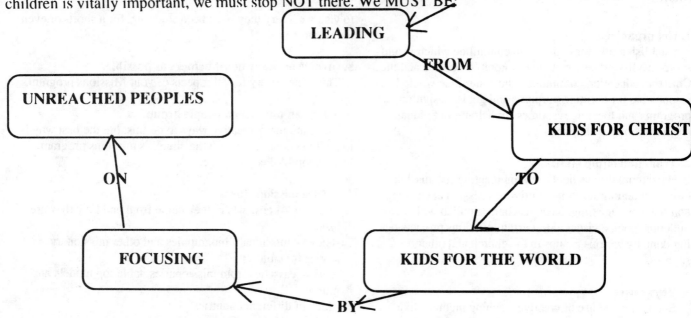

"Therefore go and make disciples of all nations." Matthew 28:19.

AIMS -
1. Each child needs to understand what "missions" means.
2. Each child must realize that "the field is the world" (Matt. 13:38).
3. Each child needs to realize that after salvation comes responsibility to share Christ with those who do not know.
4. Each child needs to eventually realize that God's will for all is—MISSIONS.

WHEN TO START ?
1. At the earliest age we have them.
2. When they can understand accepting Christ, they can be challenged with missions, specifically hidden peoples.

WHERE TO START ?
1. In the home, first of all—parents' responsibility.
2. Through the children's ministry of the church:
   V.B.S., Children's Church, Sunday School, Awanna Clubs, summer-time activities, missions conferences, etc.
3. Give 5-10 minutes each Sunday.
4. Give longer time once a month.
5. In V.B.S., give 10-15 min. daily in each department.
6. Emphasize unreached peoples. Or use the term "hidden peoples" for children.
7. Start with the Introductory Hidden Peoples Lesson.

WHAT DO WE DO TO GIVE OUR KIDS A HEART FOR MISSIONS?
MOST IMPORTANT: Create a "missions" atmosphere in all the children's departments.
1. Use map of the world, world globe, bulletin boards, artifacts, posters, pictures.
2. Establish a missionary learning center.
3. Teach "missions" on a weekly or monthly basis.
4. Use a variety of teaching methods and a variety of helper-people.
5. Teach missionary songs or choruses frequently.
6. Teach Scripture verses emphasizing missions, such as the part of Matthew 28:19 quoted above; teach GO— Mark 16:15; PRAY—Matthew 9:38; GIVE—2 Cor. 9:7, and others.
6. Use missionary stories from different lands.
7. Use a missionary speaker, or a foreign student.
8. Use a missionary biography story
9. Always use some type of visual aid
10. "Show and Tell."
11. Do "tape-sponding" with a selected missionary and have children sing and talk on tape.
   -Use one tape to send back and forth.
   -Encourage missionary to list prayer requests, describe local life, sing local songs, have their children talk and sing.
   -Have the children's group pray for the requests, then talk and sing on the tape.

12. Use the "Hidden Peoples Introductory Lesson," as one of the first lessons.
13. Teach and encourage the "Adopt-A-People" concept (see "Adopt-A-People" article).
14. Learn simple songs in a foreign language which the missionary has used.
15. If using the Children's Church time, an on-going missionary adventure story can be used, telling a chapter or episode each Sunday. Any curriculum in this book could be used. Arouse anticipated excitement for the next episode.
16. Have occasional slide-shows or videos.
17. Have occasional puppet plays or skits.
18. Have ethnic snacks and games. Sometimes the games can have an acting-out of the story.
19. Play games using an inflatable world globe and finding countries and people groups.
20. Take an artifact or curio in a paper bag and create suspense.
21. As children become familiar with the missionaries and agencies supported by the church, have quizzes about them.
22. Have quizzes and games involving going to the hidden peoples.
23. Keep the children informed of prayer requests.
    -Write requests on slips of paper. Let one person draw, and pray.
    -Let each child draw one to take home and pray all week.
24. Emphasize stewardship—encourage children to give their own money.
    -suggest ways they may earn money themselves.
    -motivate their giving by setting department goals for specific needs.
    -if the church stresses "Faith Promise" giving, use a "Faith Promise" plan for children.
25. Stimulate them to be "missionaries" now—with stories of others
26. Encourage "pen-pals"— with M.K.'s on the field.
27. Have a children's missions conference during the church's regular missions conference.
28. Have a missions fair during a missions conference, or separately. There are many ideas for this.
29. Use the *Global Prayer Digest* regularly, reading either the children's (Sunday) stories, or any of the stories appropriate for children.
30. Pre-school, first and second grades can adopt an MK to correspond with and pray for.
31. Have a "get-away" missions retreat for kids in grades five and up. This is a NEW and TERRIFIC idea. Get the basic "Jr. Mission Retreat" curriculum from One Way Street (see PUBLISHERS), and add to it with creative ideas.

REMEMBER—God will use your heart as you give all your heart, enthusiasm and involvement in missions make this attitude contagious in children.

HOW TO GIVE KIDS A HEART?

1. Have a "missions co-ordinator" for all the children's ministries.
   - gather information and materials, perhaps making a "library" of materials.
   - collect artifacts and curios (missionaries can cooperate with this).
   - gather "source" material (get ideas from this book).
2. Have a "missions corresponding secretary."
3. Have a "missions story-teller," or have a list of volunteers who will take turns doing this.
4. Have a special "Hidden Peoples" Sunday.
   - children come in costumes (may make simple costumes in class over a period of several classes).
   - practice and put on a play with or without costumes.
   - enlist mothers to help with the costumes.
   - use puppets, if desired, for plays.
   - have a special slide show or video.
   - prepare pin-on tags for the children designating they are members of the "Hidden Peoples" Club.
   - have a "hidden peoples" loose change jar for the class or department.
   - give "hidden peoples" jar labels to each child who promises to have a loose change jar at home with his family.
5. Make one large poster for each of the five major people group blocks—TRIBAL, MUSLIM, HINDU, CHINESE and BUDDHIST.
   - use colorful tag-board to mount colorful pictures, such as those from *National Geographic* magazines.
   - use these as teaching posters.
6. Use activities, songs, crafts, visual aids and/or snacks all related to each lesson and country/culture studied.
7. Write for information when planning to "adopt" a people group (see information in "Adopt-A-People Group" article).
   - inquire whether your church or denomination mission board is targeting one or more unreached people group.
   - using the *Global Prayer Digest* will help give information leading to choose a people group.
   - send for pictures and slides about the people group you are interested in.
   - correspond with missionaries of missionary agencies focusing on that group.
   - use the money from the loose change "Hidden Peoples" jars for your people group.
8. Use the books, *Missions Ideas* and *52 Ways to Teach Missions* for many ideas on "HOW TO" (see addresses in the ACTIVITY and PUBLISHERS sections).

IS ALL THIS EFFORT WORTHWHILE?
YES!!
Ask missionaries when they first became intested in mission. Most will say, "in childhood or youth."

ADOPT-A-PEOPLE
FOR CHILDREN
A Church for Every People By the Year 2000

WHY ADOPT A PEOPLE GROUP?
It is urgent to SEE children's groups more actively involved in adopting "unreached" people groups. Children's workers need to see this as a practical and logical follow-up to children's missions education. If there are approximately 11,000 people groups in the world still to be effectively "reached," and approximately 700 churches worldwide for every people group, isn't it time we look into **HOW** children can plug into this all-out, necessary effort? Adoption is a familiar concept these days, with agencies proposing that we "adopt" everything from a tree, an endangered species, to a child in Romania. **I propose that, due to the urgency of the Great Commission given to us by God, that children not only CAN, but NEED to adopt people groups—BUT IT WILL TAKE COMMITMENT.**   - Gerry Dueck

THE TASK CAN BE DONE!

"And this Gospel of the kingdom will be preached in the whole world as a testimony to all nations. (Gk.ethne, peoples) and then the end will come." Matthew 24:14
"You were slain, and with your blood you purchased men for God from every tribe and language and people and nation." Revelation 5:9

HOW CAN WE COMPLETE THE GREAT COMMISSION?
The Reached Peoples: Today, **620 million** out of 5.4 billion people in the world are Bible-believing Christians, located in about 7 million congregations. With the rapid increase in world population, many people cannot believe that the Kingdom of Christ is expanding over three times the rate of world population growth.
The Remaing Task: **11,000** peoples do not yet have a church, and can be divided into 5 major blocks:
3,800 *Muslim* groups.
2,700 *Tribal* groups.
1,800 *Hindu* groups.
900 *Chinese* groups.
900 *Buddhist* groups.
900 *Other* people groups.
Suggestion: Think of the phrase "**M**ost **T**hat **H**eaven **C**an **B**oast **O**ver," using the bold letters for the people groups.
1. Identify the goal.
Mission agencies and researchers are busy identifying every last tribe, tongue, and people on earth where a church movement must still be planted. **An unreached people is a group within which there is no indigenous community of believing Christians with adequate numbers and resources to evangelize this people group without requiring outside (cross-cultural) assistance.**
2. Mobilize the manpower.
There are over seven million evangelical congregations of vital believers worldwide. Since there are 11,000 unreached people groups, the ratio of congregations to people groups is about 700 to one! Think of the potential of just 10 congregations united to plant a church in a single people group. Never before has Christ's church been so hopefully situated for **finishing** the task!

3. Finish the task in bite-sized pieces.
The world is too big for any one congregation to tackle. But in this final challenge to complete the task, each congregation can unite with others to adopt at least one of the 11,000 unreached people groups.
4. Involve Children.
Children's groups can either initiate or propose the adoption of a people group, challenging their church to join them; or they can join their church in the adoption of one or more groups.

WHAT DOES IT MEAN TO "ADOPT" AN UNREACHED PEOPLE GROUP?
> It means that one or more congregations or fellowship groups work through their chosen mission agencies to provide informed, dedicated prayer and financial support for a specific unreached people group.
> It means maintaining that commitment until a growing evangelizing church movement is established within this unreached people group.

WHY YOUR CHILDREN'S GROUP AND/OR YOUR CHURCH SHOULD ADOPT AN UNREACHED PEOPLE GROUP

We adopt people groups because **they are in bondage to Satan and need to be free.** People need the Lord! Our focus is on bringing the gospel to **peoples.** Our focus is not on what adopting can do for our children, even though it can bring a blessing; rather it is on passing the blessing of being part of God's family on to others. **We are actually helping a people to be adopted into God's family.**

IMPORTANT CONCEPTS for seeing a people group adopted into God's family—you need to know:
a) **a proper name for that group**
b) **a location of significant numbers of that group**
- a people group meets one or more of the following:
  1) The people group has not heard.
  2) The people group has not responded.
  3) The people group does not have a church.
  4) The people group does not have the Word of God translated into their mother tongue.

WHAT CAN YOUR CHILDREN'S GROUP DO NOW?

1. Make Contact!

> First explore adopting an unreached people together with your church and/or your denominational mission headquarters, mission agency,or select an agency you have worked with. If your congregation does not have such a link, then the best place to look up a people group is in *Operation World* by Patrick Johnstone.

> If your church has a specific geographic area or people group in mind, you can ask for information and suggestions from the Adopt-a-People Campaign Office, at U.S. Center for World Mission. They will point you to the agencies whose plans are close to what your goals are. They have resources available for churches to use.

2. Obtain the Resources:

>**Study your people group** by getting all the resources from the agencies and others you can find yourself, including *National Geographic* and *Global Prayer Digest*, and using this in teaching the children. Write the Adopt-a-People Clearinghouse for "People Profiles."

3. Regular Focus

> Dicuss and **pray for them** every time you meet together (Ex.: every S.S. session). In order for your church to join you in studying your people group, praying for them, and setting the goals, **suggest that your church order the *Doing Your Bit* dramatic 10-minute video, the *Adopt-a-People Advocate Kit*, or the book, *Adoption: A Practical Guide to Sudessfully Adopting an Unreached People Group*.** You can order these by calling or writing William Carey Library Publishers (see address below).

4. Collect loose change for them

> Route it to a missionary agency targeting them.

5. Use Materials Focused on Unreached Peoples

> Develop your vision for the unreached by motivating and educating both your children's groups and your church, using curriculum that focuses on unreached people groups.

> Obtain and regularly use the *Global Prayer Digest* yourself and with the children (use USCWM address).

6. Equip your Church to do their part by getting the Adopt-A-People Resources from the addresses given.

- - - - - - - - - - - - -

REMEMBER, THE HEART OF THE ADOPT-A-PEOPLE CONCEPT IS THE LINKING OF A LOCAL CONGREGATION WITH A SPECIFIC UNREACHED PEOPLE GROUP, WORKING THROUGH A MISSION AGENCY.

- - - - - - - - - -

Go ahead—take a people group to heaven with you!

SUGGESTED IDEAS TO USE ADOPT-A-PEOPLE WITH CHILDREN

1) Introduce the "unreached peoples" concept to the children by using the "Hidden Peoples Introductory Lesson" (available from Children's Missions Resource Center).

2) Introduce the "Adoption" concept to them by telling them a story about adoption of a child. What principles involved are the same?

3) Have a bulletin board exclusively for your "adopted people group." Fill it with pictures and any other information. Encourage the children to collect things and share them.

4) Have some kind of focus concerning your "people group" every Sunday (or whenever you meet), even if only 5 minutes.

5) Teach them how to pray for their "group."

6) Make a scrapbook about your people group, using a photo album with plastic-covered pages. Use articles, pictures, etc.

7) Find out how your people group dresses, and make simple costumes. Have special Sundays when children come dressed in the costumes. Put on a play with the children or a with puppets.

8) Find out what your people group eats, and make and eat some ethnic snacks.

9) Introduce loose change container, label it with your people group name. You might even have a contest with some sort of creative poster depicting your people group.

10) Adopt the children of your people group.

11) Find out if there are already missionaries going to your group, and have children correspond with them. Sending tapes back and forth is a wonderful idea.

12) For more ideas or materials write CMRC , 1605 Elizabeth St., Pasadena CA 91104.

FOR YOUR VISUAL AID TEACHING:
GET BEAUTIFUL 5"X7" PEOPLE GROUP CARDS
Seven cards are now available with a photo on the front and inside is a brief profile of the people group, a simple map, and facts about the group.Wonderful small tool to have children (or adults) learn to pray for unreached people groups. Most of the color photographs are of children. Assorted 5-pack is $5.75 (discount); 10-pack of one people group is $11.50 (discount). Available are: **Bihari, Fulani, Kashmari, Thai, Turkman, Uighurs, and Uzbeks.** Order from William Carey Library (address below) and include $2.00 S & H.

WE WANT TO SEE EVERY UNREACHED PEOPLE BATHED IN DAILY PRAYER, ADOPTED IN LOVE, AND TARGETED BY CULTURALLY-SENSITIVE AND COMMITTED CHRISTIANS.

William Carey Library, P.O. Box 40129, Pasadena, CA 91114. Phone(818)798-0819 or 1-800-MISSION (for orders only).

Mobilization Division, U.S. Center for World Mission, 1605 Elizabeth St, Pasadena, CA 91104. (818) 398-2200.

Adopt-A-People Clearinghouse, 721 N. Tejon,Ccolorado Springs, CO 80903. (719) 473-8800;.FAX 719-473-5907.